DATE DUE

JUN 1 2 2003			

MAURO IN AMERICA

Mauro in America

An Italian Artist Visits the New World

Mimi Cazort

Transcription and Translation

by Antonia Reiner Franklin

with Mimi Cazort

Yale University Press

New Haven & London

Designed by Sandy Chapman

Printed in China

Library of Congress Cataloging-in-Publication Data

Gandolfi, Mauro, 1764–1834.
[Viaggio agli Stati Uniti. English]
Mauro in America : an Italian artist visits the new world / Mimi
Cazort ; translation by Antonia Reiner Franklin.
p. cm.
Includes bibliographical references and index.
ISBN 0-300-09221-0
1. Gandolfi, Mauro, 1764–1834–Journeys–United States. 2. United
States--Description and travel. I. Cazort, Mimi. II. Title.
N6923.G3498 A2 2003
917.304'51--dc21
2002014614

Frontispiece   Detail of fig. 9.
Page vi   Detail of fig. 38.
Page. viii   Detail of fig. 49.

Contents

Acknowledgments

vii

Introduction

"My Sacred Principle of Independence"

Mauro Gandolfi's Voyage to the United States in 1816

1

Voyage to the United States of America

Undertaken by Mauro Gandolfi in the year 1816

47

Notes

119

Bibliography

144

List of Illustrations

149

Index

153

Acknowledgments

In 1816 the Bolognese painter and printmaker Mauro Gandolfi decided to try his fortunes in the New World. The manuscript account of his trip, the "Viaggio agli Stati Uniti" has been referred to in the literature but has never before been fully transcribed and published, either in Italian or in translation. The problem was not one of accessibility: its custodians at the Cassa di Risparmio in Bologna have made it available on request to anyone interested. The problem was more likely one of legibility.

Mauro's original manuscript, which would have been penned in the elegant script of the professional engraver as we know it from his letters, had remained with the Gandolfi family until 1944 when it disappeared, along with other family papers, under the Allied bombing of Bologna. Antonia Reiner Franklin and I have worked from the manuscript copy made by the Bolognese writer Michelangelo Gualandi in 1843. This copy, though conscientious and accurate, was apparently written in haste and thus difficult to decipher.

Mauro chose the epistolary form for his memoir, addressing it to an unidentified friend. The spontaneous nature of his observations and the abbreviated and sometimes breathless quality of his prose are well-suited to this format. He had no interest in philosophies of government or political theories about this New Republic he had set out to explore but rather, as an artist, was content to make verbal sketches of the places he chose to visit. He arranged his comments thematically, prefacing his subsections with subtitles. Like his hasty pen sketches, the sections vary in scope and specificity. Some are succinct one liners, some meander along a stream of consciousness that will depart unexpectedly from the subject as initially declared. In line with our decision to render Mauro's text as closely as possible, we have maintained his sudivisions and subtitles and inclined toward a literal translation. To illustrate the scenes Mauro described I have chosen prints and drawings by other travellers of the period, the sketches Mauro made on the trip having been destroyed along with the original manuscript.

I have written an introduction outlining the Bolognese artistic tradition of which Mauro was the product. The fragmentation of opportunity for artists occasioned by the incursion of the French into Italy in 1796 led to his learning the engraver's trade in Paris and setting out for a life in the New World. I have illustrated this section with examples of Mauro's other work in painting, drawing, and printmaking selected to convey facets of his concerns as an artist. In the end, neither his personality or his skills proved compatible with his expectations of the New World, or the New World's expectations of him.

I would like to the friends and colleagues who have aided me in this enterprise. First, of course, my colleague in the transcription and translation, Antonia Reiner Franklin. Italian associates have been unstinting in their support: Franca Varignana, Anna Maria Scardovi, Adriano Cera, Eugenio Riccomani and Fabrizio Apolloni. Essential assistance for the history and illustrations of New York and Philadelphia was generously provided by Wendy Shadwell, Darrell Sewell, Bea Garvin, Sara Weatherwax, Roberta Waddell and Alan Stone. The editors at Yale University Press provided gentle guidance throughout.

I would like to dedicate the book to the memory of my husband, Robert Alexander McLarty.

Mimi Cazort

Introduction

"My Sacred Principle of Independence"

Mauro Gandolfi's Voyage to the United States in 1816

On 11 April 1816 Mauro Gandolfi, fifty-two years old and a painter and engraver by trade, set sail from Bordeaux on the merchant brigadier *William and Henry*. He had obtained first class passage for himself and his mistress, Teresa Diani, for 1,600 francs.[1] The fare included their personal effects, three trunks of clothes, and a case of engravings intended for gift or sale. He was pleased that they would be seated at Captain Almy's table, and smugly commented in his memoirs of the trip, the "Viaggio agli Stati Uniti (Voyage to the United States) 1816," that though the other passengers lodged below deck had paid less, they were bound to suffer more.[2] After a crossing of thirty-five days, the ship arrived in New York.[3] Mauro informed the reader that his passport was in order, and pointedly noted that he had taken the precaution of altering his name slightly for the Customs Officials to "Mr. Moro and his wife" in order to confound some Bolognese slanderer who might be out to sully his reputation. Our attention is arrested: what or whom was this man fleeing?

Mauro Gandolfi (18 September 1764 – 4 January 1834) penned the account of his trip to America in Milan in 1822, six years after his return to Italy.[4] His story appeals to the modern reader on several counts. It is succinct, and affords us a series of snap-shot impressions of the places he visited. It also bears the unmistakable stamp of authenticity. His detailed citations of names and street addresses, architecture, and theatrical events indicate that he took notes during his stay and worked up his "Voyage" from these. A check of these facts has proved them correct. A witty and perceptive observer, he scorns the supercilious attitude of some later and more famous travellers such as Frances Trollope or Charles Dickens.[5] He had neither the credentials nor the pretensions of being an historian or a political philosopher, in contrast to Alexis de

Tocqueville who, writing in 1835, was positioned to expound on such matters. Mauro arrived with his beliefs in democratic principles and a republican form of government already firmly entrenched, and sought to prove their viability by witnessing the United States at first hand. A comparison of his account with an earlier and much longer travelogue by another cosmopolitan Italian, the botanist Luigi Castiglione, reveals the intensely personal character of Mauro's observations.[6] Castiglione travelled the northeast of the United States and as far south as Georgia between 1785 and 1787 and noted primarily the geography, topography, history, and botany of the country. He seemed impervious, however, to the quirks of human nature that so fascinated Mauro. Mauro was above all an artist, and it was as an artist that he recorded his impressions. His observations are curiously unpremeditated, and the absence of preconceived expectations contributes to their charm. One only wishes that he had written more and expanded his comments in greater detail.

In July 1834, seven months after Mauro's death, Michelangelo Gualandi, a Bolognese literary and art critic and author of a guide book on Bologna,[7] borrowed the original manuscript from Clementina (Mauro's daughter) and made a copy that he sent to his and Mauro's mutual friend Luciano Scarabelli, urging him to try to get it published. His prefatory notes addressed to Scarabelli state that he had made the copy diligently with no textual alterations. Scarabelli finally arranged for publication in 1842 in the literary weekly newspaper *Il vaglio: Giornale critico, scientifico, artistico, letterario* to which he was a frequent contributor, along with a short biographical note on the artist.[8] In July 1866 Scarabelli, by then Professor of Aesthetics at the University of Bologna, sent the copy back to Gualandi. It was later acquired by the Cassa di Risparmio in Bologna where it remains today. It is the Gualandi-Scarabelli copy that is presented here.

The original signed manuscript of the "Voyage" and numerous other family papers and documents came down through the Gandolfi family to the Bolognese physician Dr. Augusto Zanotti, the great-grandson of Clementina.[9] All of the original material preserved by the family was lost in the Allied bombing of Bologna in July 1944 including, most regrettably, the drawings he described in his manuscript as having made.[10] Dr. Zanotti did not include the "Voyage" in his 1925 publication of Mauro's autobiography, written in 1833 shortly before his death, but he described it and its previous partial publications, oddly omitting Scarabelli's. Zanotti praised the brief extracts published between 1905 and 1907 in the Bolognese newspaper *Il resto del carlino* which were evidently submitted by a friend and doubtless from the original manuscript in Zanotti's possession. He spoke with some disdain of the longer (and somewhat embroidered) extract that appeared in 1906–7 in the Catholic journal *L'Avvenire d'Italia*.

The "Voyage" was composed as a series of letters and written in a single month, the June of 1822. It was addressed to an unnamed recipient in Milan identified only as "amico carissimo." It is not known whether Mauro actually intended these to be sent as letters, or if he simply made use of the epistolary convention to allow him to recount his mid-life adventure in the hope of having it published.[11] We assume that Mauro himself devised the arrangement of the text into the chronological and topical sections that we have retained with a few minor adjustments for continuity. We have translated the text as literally as possible, maintaining Mauro's informal style replete with exclamations of amazement, delight, or chagrin and his tendency to move back and forth from observation to generalization.

Mauro's French was fluent and he sought out fellow francophones. His contacts with other Americans seem to have been somewhat casual and transitory, which may have been due to his faulty English, shown by his comical transcriptions of names and places. He was not taken up socially by the prominent American artists of the day such as Thomas Sully and the Peales. Instead he sought out fellow craftsmen and dealers in *objets d'art*, immigrants like himself. This choice of humbler company gave him insights into the everyday world of the new country's two main cities, insights unfiltered through the eyes of official image-makers, as active then as now. He seems to have developed particular friendships with French-speaking immigrants in Philadelphia where the citizens, all agog after 1787 at the revolutionary developments in France, had welcomed émigrés, many of whom, like Dupont de Nemours, were to remain in the area.[12]

A brief look at Mauro's life and circumstances will put the "Voyage" into perspective and clarify his motives for undertaking the trip in the first place. From the available biographical data and Mauro's own written words, a patchwork image emerges of a man at odds with himself as well as with his time and place, but though vain and pugnacious he retains an irresistible appeal. He was the eldest of eight children of Giovanna Spisani and Gaetano Gandolfi (1734–1802), the leading artist of late eighteenth-century Bologna.[13] He described his childhood in the brief manuscript autobiography that Zanotti published in 1925 (fig. 1).[14]

Mauro was torn between choosing a career as an artist or as a musician. His father had tried to discourage him from becoming an artist, saying it would be a hard life, and in any case after the boy reached the age of fourteen the family would no longer maintain him as they had so many mouths to feed. Nevertheless, he decided to "make art my inseparable consort and music my mistress," perhaps a metaphor of his connubial ambivalence which later became a reality.[15] At the age of ten he began to study painting seriously, and in the autobiography told us how he learned to draw: "And seeing how my

1   Gaetano Gandolfi, *Portrait of Mauro at Age Four*, 1768, oil on canvas.

father passed the early hours of the winter evenings near the fireplace sketching out those famous pen drawings of his, I would sneak out of bed furtively and pass the better part of the night copying them with such diligence that one day he himself wasn't sure which was the original and which the copy."[16] According to his story, his two passions, "for the beautiful and for love," prompted an unrequited ardour for a local girl that began when he was only nine and prompted his first "viaggio" in 1782 when, at age eighteen, he ran away from home to France, remaining there for five years.[17] This escapade foreshadowed his transatlantic voyage almost forty years later.

The posthumous account of Mauro's life by his friend Luciano Scarabelli substantiates the tale: "In his youth he took a notion to travel, driven by the desperation of love. He was only sixteen years old when a girl whom he loved passionately turned her back on him. He sought out as travelling companion one of his father's students, and they set off together one fine day after sundown, taking little money but lots of drawings.[18]

Mauro's autobiographical account of the two boys' adventures is highly colored and romantic, but lacks the tone of veracity one finds in "Voyage." They crossed the Appenines and reached Sestri on the Ligurian coast where the sight of the sea "struck us speechless with wonder." They took a ship, and an old woman taught them a successful remedy for seasickness.[19] Bit by bit they made their way on foot to Marseilles, arriving with only a few coins and Mauro's drawings. Here they were accosted by two officials with the Royal Corsican Regiment: "And why, my fine young men, since you're so handsome, don't you join us?" Which they promptly did, with the proviso that they would be released as soon as they were able to pay back the sum advanced to them. Once enlisted Mauro let it slip that he was an artist whereupon a soldier requested an image of St. Anthony. A St. Anthony was duly produced.[20]

The Regiment was transferred away from Strasbourg in August 1782. Mauro then replaced his fleeting military career with a two-year attachment to an Italian maker of bibelots and decorative objects, one Francesco Saverio Adorno. A Bolognese legal document describes how in 1783 Mauro's father was obliged to pay three hundred lire to guarantee that the young man would serve out his six-year apprenticeship.[21] Mauro, ever mobile, apparently skipped out on his contractual obligations, but his brief artisanal training with Adorno may have sensitized him to precision of detail, a characteristic of all his later work. He would surely have been enchanted by his master's other accomplishment, which occurred during his period of apprenticeship: in 1784 Adorno successfully launched a hot air balloon over Strasbourg, only one year after the Montgolfier brothers' triumph in Paris. Mauro then spent two years at Arras and a final period in Paris in 1787. It was probably during this time

2 Mauro Gandolfi, *The Cistern of the Palazzo Pubblico, Bologna, with Vagabonds at Rest*, date unknown, pen, brown ink, and wash over black chalk.

that he was exposed to the revolutionary ideas then fomenting in France that were subsequently to inform his political activity in Bologna.

What Mauro was to term "mio santo sistema d'independenza" ("my sacred principle of independence") was already evident, and his taste for travel firmly established. He returned to Bologna in 1787, his wanderlust temporarily satisfied (or his pockets empty) (fig. 2). He lived with his parents until 1789, when he set up a painting studio of his own in the Palazzo Bentivoglio, a rambling old city palace occupied by several families. An enigmatic painting that he did after his return may have been intended to commemorate his earlier flight (fig. 3). It shows a young traveller bidding a melodramatic farewell to his home while two ancients mourn his departure. The four urchins tussling on the ground could be his four brothers, one standing girls his sister Marta, and the other, who weeps inconsolably, suggests Mauro's revenge on the girl who spurned his attentions.

His first major commissions after his return were not, however, for paintings but for three ceremonial carriages for local aristocratic families in 1789, thus signalling an unusual vote of confidence for a twenty-five-year-old unproven artist with no academic credentials. In his autobiography he describes the carriage he produced for Senator Carlo Caprara Montecuccoli, saying that he not only painted its elegant side-panels but also designed the bronze and gilt-wood ornaments, which may reflect his experience with the Strasbourg artisan.[22] He finished the work in a mere three months, noting that craftsmen in Turin or Rome needed two years to complete such a project.[23] Two other carriage commissions followed for the family of Marchese Sebastiano Tanari (fig. 4).[24] A study for the allegorical figure representing

3   Mauro Gandolfi, *The Farewell*, c.1788, oil on canvas.

4   Mauro Gandolfi, *Carriage of the Tanari Family, with "Calypso Receiving Telemachus and Mentor"*, c.1789, oil on panel, gilded wood.

astronomy on one of the panels stands as the first dateable drawing we have by Mauro (fig. 5). These monumental art objects were not intended for everyday travel but for the ceremonial parades that threaded their way at appointed intervals through the piazzas and narrow alleyways of the city to mark the election of a new set of Gonfalionieri, the Senators who chose each other to the post every two months. The Gonfalionieri had no real power at this point and the purpose of their processionals was pure ostentation. They served also as a pleasant occasions for universal festivity. Mauro's astonished observations at the Fourth of July parade in New York that no distinctions of rank were visible in people's dress, and where giant images of republican virtue were hauled through the streets instead of aristocrats framed by gilded putti, must be seen in this context.

Following his early success, Mauro was enrolled from 1791 to 1792 in the school of the Accademia Clementina, the chief teaching institution for artists in Emilia-Romagna. As was true of most academies of the period, the Clementina functioned also as trade union, financial agency, and burial soci-

5   Mauro Gandolfi, *Allegory of Astronomy*, c.1789, pen, brown ink, and blue, rose, yellow, and brown washes over black chalk.

ety for its artists.[25] It maintained a stranglehold on painting commissions in the city which meant that enrollment at its school was obligatory for professional advancement. The standards maintained by the school, as well as Mauro's extraordinary facility in drawing from the nude, are confirmed by two splendid black chalk nude drawings that are bound into albums dated 1791 and 1792 containing the studies from life deemed annually by the instructors to be the most worthy (fig. 6).[26] Their superb quality underlies the impassioned plea that Mauro voiced in his "Voyage" for this kind of training.

On 16 February 1792, the year he completed his formal training, Mauro took a wife,[27] the fifteen-year-old Laura Zanetti whom he describes affectionately in his autobiography as being, like him, a singer and equally devoted to music.[28] A son, Raffaele, was born nine months later but died in 1811 at age nineteen of wounds suffered with Napoleon's army in Spain.[29] A daughter, appropriately named Clementina, was born in January 1795.[30] She was to remain Mauro's pride and joy and is mentioned frequently in his letters and in his Testamento. He inscribed her name on an idealized etched portrait in

6   Mauro Gandolfi, *Seated male nude*, 1792, black chalk heightened with white.

7   Mauro Gandolfi, *Clementina*, date unknown, etching.

which she wears an improbable English-style hat (fig. 7). Mauro stated that after "three years of paradise," Laura died in early 1795, soon after Clementina's birth, while he was away on a trip to Rome.[31]

Two painted self-portraits indicate the discrepant sides of Mauro's personality that become evident in reading his "Voyage": the independent thinker and the worldly *bon vivant* (figs. 8 and 9). The first shows a handsome and self-assured young man, roughly costumed as a budding revolutionary.[32] The painting is neither signed nor dated and was at one time attributed to Mauro's father, Gaetano, though the monochromatic palette is closer to Mauro.[33] Attribution questions aside (and confusion between the hands of son and father persist), the question of its date remains. Does it show Mauro at age eighteen, just before his leap into vagabondage? This interpretation would be in line with the young man's own self-image, precociously romantic.

The second painting shows a quite different self-appraisal. Mauro is fashionably dressed in the French manner, and his hair is powdered: the young revolutionary has become a man of the world. The painting, currently in the Pinacoteca Nazionale di Bologna, was originally in the collection of the Accademia Clementina.[34] It was probably presented to the Accademia on the occasion of Mauro's election to that body in 1794, as was customary. He represents himself as a confident young artist, his palette and brushes set aside for the moment, tuning his guitar.

After Mauro was elected to the Accademia, he was nominated Direttore di Figura (instructor in figure drawing) on 4 October 1797 and again on 13 October 1800.[35] In the early 1790s Mauro's career as a painter reached its peak. He stated frankly in his autobiography that he was active as a painter for only ten years, from 1786 to 1796, that "there was a total lack of major artistic projects due to the suppression of the convents and the empty coffers of the rich."[36] The mainstay of artists throughout the Papal States had been religious commissions, but propagandizing the faith had slowed to a trickle owing to

8   Mauro Gandolfi, *Self-Portrait as a Young Man*, *c*.1782, oil on canvas.

9 Mauro Gandolfi, *Self-Portrait at Age Thirty*, 1794, oil on canvas.

10   Mauro Gandolfi, *St. Dominic Burning the Books*, 1790, oil on canvas.

the suppressions, the Church's internal inertia, and economic and political pressures from the outside. Nonetheless, in 1790 the Domenicans (whose mother church was in Bologna), requested from the Gandolfi a triad of large altarpieces portraying episodes from the life of their titular saint, for a chapel in their vast church in Ferrara.[37] Gaetano executed the central painting and Mauro the other two. The scale of the commission, issued a mere five years before the Domenicans were suppressed, suggests a final gesture of militant defiance on the part of the Order in the face of its imminent demise.

11   Mauro Gandolfi, *St. Francis and the Pilgrims*, c.1790, oil on canvas.

St. Dominic Burning the Books, one of Mauro's contributions, is surely one of the oddest in all his exotic religious oeuvre (fig. 10). A central compositional element is the obscenely obese belly of an irrelevant Turk who leers at the drama, watched in turn by a snickering girl. Does the Turk's smug smile suggest pleasure at the destruction of Western cultural artifacts, in which case the saint has been deftly co-opted by the forces of Islam? It is inconceivable that Mauro, fired as he was by Enlightenment thinking, could take the patently unenlightened subject of book-burning seriously, and one suspects an element of satire in his representation.

The Dominican painting was not a unique case. Mauro continued to slyly interpose secular and often frankly sensual elements into his religious compositions, though he did not always get away with it. When asked around 1792 to produce an altar frontal for the little church annexed to the Ospedale di San Francesco, an ancient hospital established to care for pilgrims of the Order of St. Francis, he produced an astonishing bozzetto, or oil sketch (fig. 11). The personage of the "pilgrim" is represented by a pretty girl in a fashionable bonnet who eyes us seductively, seemingly bored by the saintly Francis .[38] In the finished painting, as installed with the approval of the Franciscans, the little beauty has changed sex, changed attitude, and become St. James the Pilgrim, his eyes fixed adoringly on Saint Francis.[39] In like manner, Mauro's preparatory drawing for the painting *The Healing Vision of St. Pellegrino Laziosi*, done for the the church of the Servites in Rimini, verges on the comic (fig. 12). The finished painting has settled into acceptable conventionality.[40]

Mauro's ironic treatment of sacrosanct subjects, apparently a kind of private joke, may have been a factor in the falling off of his commissions, but his

12   Mauro Gandolfi, *The Healing Vision of St. Pellegrino Laziosi*, date unknown, pen, brown ink, and brown wash.

tribulations as an artist in Italy at the end of the eighteenth century did not constitute an isolated event. Napoleonic decrees after 1796 had closed not only the churches, monasteries, and convents but also the ecclesiastically sponsored foundations for social welfare: the *Opere Pie*. These institutions ranged from homes for unwed mothers, battered wives, and girls without dowries, to separate orphanages for male and female, legitimate and illegitimate orphans, and hospices for the infirm, the old, and the occasional sick traveller. The inmates depended on devotional images for their spiritual well-being and instruction, and the insatiable demands for these had constituted the bread of life for Bolognese artists.[41] When the flow of commissions dried up, the destabilizing effect on the artistic community in Bologna, the "Second Papal City" of Italy, was profound. It produced a situation of special poignancy for Mauro, who, though he had enthusiastically endorsed the dismantling of church, state, and social hierarchy, found himself adrift in a world that lacked an employment structure. On the secular front, the nobility and wealthy bourgeoisie were deprived of their spending power. Although class warfare and social turmoil were far less tumultuous in Italy than in France, the production of portraits, palace decorations, and ceremonial carriages ground to a halt.

With the end of his painting career, Mauro seems to have substituted political involvement for artistic endeavour. His sympathy with the republican cause is well documented. He was initially supportive of Napoleon, hoping with many of his liberal contemporaries that the ancient church–aristocracy consortium that had controlled the city's internal affairs for three centuries would at last be abolished. On 3 September 1796 he led the group who welcomed Napoleon into Bologna, "all citizens and not one nobleman,"

13   Mauro Gandolfi, *Repubblica Cisalpina*, c.1797, etching.

claiming to be admirably suited for this task as he spoke fluent French.[42] The proclamation of the Cispadane Republic occasioned a grand *festa* in the Piazza Maggiore with two orchestras playing around the Tree of Liberty and appropriate decorations, all designed by Mauro.[43] The next big event was the celebration of the fall of Mantua to Napoleonic forces on 16 February 1797 and again Mauro obliged: "That spectacle, so well conceived, was orchestrated by our noted citizen, Mauro Gandolfi, who managed it all in twelve hours!"[44]

In the same year he was invited to submit a design for the new uniforms of the Cispadane Republic and later was commissioned to design the first flag of the Republic, whose distinctive green, white, and red bands constitute the Italian flag today.[45] The uniforms and flags have gone the way of most objects of material history, but some examples of Mauro's etchings for revolutionary ephemera remain. These prints are rarely found today as they were made to be used and discarded. A small group recently came to light, including one whose inscription indicates that it was intended as an "assegnato," or official government scrip.[46] It is registered in the name of the Cisalpine Republic by Count Caprara, whose family had commissioned Mauro's early carriage decoration (fig. 13). Another shows Liberty seated under her eponymous Tree, a Phrygian hat balanced on her staff and the towers of Bologna in the distance, clearly illustrating Mauro's allegiances.

After Napoleon dismantled the religious institutions, the municipality inherited the responsibility for social services such as feeding the poor, and Mauro, patriotic citizen that he was, took part in a number of these. His prominence in his own city is shown by the municipal causes in which he was involved. He was the director of public spectacles for three years, served as a Justice of the Peace and as the inspector of theatres and of hospitals in the outlying areas, performing these functions without remuneration.[47] These experiences in civic activism shed light on his interest, both from the social and the architectural points of view, in the theatres, hospitals, and prisons of the New World as described in his "Voyage."

We catch faint echos of Mauro's dedication to his new role as civic man of action in a contemporary's account of the realization of the great new cemetery in Bologna. According to Giovanni Zecchi, an early historian of the cemetery, in 1797 Mauro Gandolfi, "a citizen member of the Municipal Government guided by love of the Fatherland and a zealous promoter of anything that could redound to the public good,"[48] proposed to revive a moribund Senatorial decree of 1784 that had mandated the construction of four new cemeteries outside the city walls to correspond with the four quarters of the city. Mauro revised this over-ambitious plan, but his suggestion of a single cemetery met with opposition until he delivered a written building proposal complete with a drawn plan, based on the geometrically laid out French cemeteries he had observed during his youthful travels in that country.[49] His site recommendation was the vast grounds of the deconsecrated monastery of the Certosini, outside the Porta Saragozza. He had embarked on the tedious process of fund-raising when, according to the above mentioned authority, he was called to Paris for an important commission, though, as we will see below, the reason he abandoned the project was more likely an insoluble domestic entanglement. The paucity of commissions that Mauro deplored is attested by the fact that many of his talented colleagues including Filippo Pedrini, Pietro Fancelli, and Flaminio Minozzi were reduced to manufacturing hack frescos for the loggias of the new cemetery. The Certosa remains intact today, a trove of nineteenth-century necropolis decor.

Mauro's involvement in public causes declined as he realized that French hegemony was not a passing event, a mere step toward the establishment of an independent Italian republic.[50] Along with many other idealistic Italians, he came to realize that the heroic young French general who had defeated the old regime and promised to respect the autonomy of his conquered territory was busily at work looting Italian art. Freedom from Church and State was an illusion that receded daily.

Mauro was one of the forty-two members elected to the First Cispadane Congress, the result of French-imposed electoral reforms. The Congress met in Modena from the 16th to the 18th of October 1796.[51] The Cispadane Republic that it proclaimed, however, existed officially only from February to July 1797. It was then supplanted by the Cisalpine Republic, whose members were less independent and more in sympathy with Napoleon's dynastic ambitions as well as his rapprochement with the Church, a direction that alienated Mauro's affections. According to Gandolfi family legend, Mauro's belief in Napoleon soured when the Emperor abdicated on 23 June 1815 in favor of his infant son, whom he had proclaimed the King of Rome. It is more likely that Mauro's disillusionment had begun earlier, occasioned by the Emperor's imposition in 1805 of the "Statuto Costituzionale," which allowed him to assume the crown of Italy for himself, distributing subsidiary authority to members of his family and appointees. The final blow to Mauro's illusions was the restoration of the old order of the Papal States in north Italy, which Napoleon had abolished in 1808, by the Congress of Vienna in 1814–15.[52] This action marked his abandonment of all his hopes for an Italian republic, and probably stimulated his hopes to see the successful American example.

Parallel to these external events, Mauro's private life entered a downward spiral. In September 1795 he had married Caterina Delpino and their son, Democrito, was born on 20 October 1796.[53] By 1798 Caterina had begun a suit for legal separation, now possible under the new Napoleonic legal codes, thus inaugurating a nasty feud which lasted several decades and which Caterina periodically revived. Her charges of abuse at Mauro's hands were dramatic and were addressed by her attorney to the Justice of the Peace, a position that, ironically, Mauro had previously held. It is impossible now to verify or disprove any of this, but the lawyer went on to caution the Justice to "call upon all your delicacy and prudence. We are dealing with a man [Mauro] who from past experience gives us reason to fear that if the proper precautions are disregarded, would heap on his poor wife all the residue of his own indignation, being inflamed by hatred at the steps, normal though they be, that she herself has taken."[54] The Justice, convinced that Mauro was a menace, ruled against him. Although the scandal of his private life had not seriously affected his professional standing (in October 1800 he was again nominated Direttore di Figura at the Accademia[55]), it is clear that public opinion was turning against him.

At this point Mauro again shifted his focus, this time from political involvement back to the production of art, and sensibly decided to develop his skills as a printmaker. The Gandolfi had always dabbled in line etching which, being simply an extension of drawing, suited their temperaments as draughtsmen. Mauro had doubtless learned the craft from his father and uncle. We know that by the spring of 1798 he had established his own printing shop in a part of the Palazzo Comunale conveniently vacated by the now defunct

Papal guard.[56] At that period such shops survived largely on the production of etched ephemera such as *cartes de visite* and letterheads. Social satire and political caricature, a mainstay of the popular press in England, never gained a firm foothold in Italy.

Mauro soon realized that a better living was to be had from reproductive engraving, and in 1800 he moved to Paris to learn this arduous technique. His new career was financed by the Bolognese Institute for Science and the Arts, a sign that he still enjoyed influential support in his "patria".[57] His economic condition was such that he could afford to maintain his house in Bologna despite the support claims of his wife. He was also able to remain in Paris for six years, the last two accompanied by his daughter, Clementina.

The choice of Paris for this astute career move was not fortuitous. The creation of the Musée de la Révolution in 1793 marked the first official institution dedicated to the reproductive engraving of works of art in the State collections in order to provide "to the public a repertoire of prestigious compositions, perfectly suited to commercial exploitation".[58] This led to the proposal in December 1796 by the President of the Republic, Paul Barras, to establish a "Chalcographie française" to encourage further the reproductive engraving of France's great paintings as well as the masterpieces that would soon be flooding into Paris via the reliable French military transport. Barras's notion of State responsibility for image dissemination was not adopted, but the Chalcographie du Louvre was eventually launched as a purely commercial venture. Some seventy-three draughtsmen worked over a period of years to draw and engrave the several hundred plates that were published in folio format as the *Musée Français* (later the *Musée Royal*).[59]

French training in reproductive engraving was the most rigorous in the world at that time, and Mauro's assiduous study is reflected in his technique. He continued to contribute engravings to the *Musée Français* after he had completed his training, including seven for the second series between 1803 and 1824, evidence that his skill was recognized in Paris (fig. 14). Although the French production system was more or less assembly-line in style, with the original masterpiece being copied by a draughtsman and someone else engraving the plate, in many cases Mauro performed both functions (fig. 15). On a few occasions he worked these up into meticulous, jewel-like versions in watercolor on vellum. He applied his new engraving technique to his draughtsmanship in the innumerable pen sketches of imaginary heads for which he is now famous. On his return to Bologna in 1806 he apparently thrived as a printmaker, concentrating on reproductive engravings and etchings. At least eighty-six prints can now be assigned to him, but until all the vignettes, ephemera, portraits, and collaborative projects are identified, no assessment of his print production is possible.[60]

14   Mauro Gandolfi (after Cristofano Allori), *Judith with the Head of Holophernes*, 1817–24, engraving and etching.

15 Mauro Gandolfi, *Sheet of Eight Fantastic Heads*, date unknown, pen and brown ink.

This period of productivity and relative tranquillity came to an abrupt halt on 12 November 1815, as it had in 1798. Mauro's estranged wife renewed her legal prosecutions, this time suing him for failure to meet his support obligations. According to his account he had paid her way to Milan, where he also maintained living quarters as it was a more active center for print publishing; they discussed the marital impasse and Mauro attempted a reconciliation but was not successful. Caterina's legal suit against him complained of maltreatment by her husband and asked support payments "in order to terminate the oppression to which she has long been subject." Once more, we have no way of knowing whether Caterina's accusations or Mauro's protestations of innocence were true, but the courts decided once more in Caterina's favor, ordered an augmentation of her monthly support payments, and decreed that Mauro take her into his house.[61] Unfortunately, three days later she tried to burn it down.

The court case and its attendant publicity toppled Mauro from his pedestal as a valued and respected citizen. It also prompted his decision to try his fortunes in the New World. Curiosity alone may not have occasioned such an ambitious journey, but by the end of 1815 the scandal that rocked his tight community had produced considerable heat. His comfortable circumstances before he fell from grace are described by Scarabelli: "He was living honorably from his art and enjoyed a large property in his home town, a house, a garden that he had furnished with waterfalls and fountains, a marshland garden for aquatic plants, sculpture, antique ruins, exotic plants, and all sorts of curiosities, and joined to this he had an esteemed museum of minerology enriched with precious stones."[62] The gems he traded in New York probably represented the residue of this collection, and his detailed curiosity about the flora of the New World and his pleasure in collecting seeds surely stemmed from the experience of his own garden.

Scarabelli continues: "His adored Clementina being married, he sold everyting in order to flee the grave displeasure of his family. He cancelled his engraved plates, assembled whatever gold and gems he had salvaged from the sale of his worldly goods, turned his face toward Milan on the sixth of February 1816, and, finding there a certain Teresa Diani, a woman anxious to accompany him to faraway lands, set forth on his planned voyage to America."[63] His house at the Belvedere di Saragozza (a good address) was bought by Count Ulisse Aldrovandi, a descendent of the famed sixteenth-century naturalist.[64] This time he was leaving Bologna for good.

Mauro's domestic debacle coincided with a general malaise among Italian liberals. A recent biography of Mauro's younger contemporary Henri Beyle (Stendhal) summed up the predicament as it affected the writer:

> The collapse of Napoleonic hegemony in 1814 had been a bitter blow to the hopes of many young Italians who, even if they chafed at the heavy-handed interference of the French government machine, nevertheless saw it as a harbinger of progress in the shape of rational reform and a measure of secularization. In its place came the new orthodoxy of restored despotism, no longer personified by the benevolent sovereigns of the Ancien Regime . . . but represented instead by their largely inglorious and intellectually dim successors.[65]

Mauro's old allegiance to the principles of democracy and republicanism combined with his dream of seeking prosperity in America, anticipating by some thirty years the mass exodus of his countrymen to the United States. He apparently had enough money to travel well (as he said at the conclusion of the "Voyage," "We cut a fine figure wherever we went"). He embarked with high hopes and a palpable sense of exhilaration compounded with the sheer relief of escaping – at whatever cost – his family obligations. His adventure lasted a mere seven months. One senses that had the New World accorded him the enthusiasm he accorded it, he might have stayed.

Mauro's tone changes unconsciously as he proceeds from the Old World to the New and back again. He launches into his "Voyage" with an account of the circuitous route that took him and his mistress Teresa from Milan to Bordeaux, their port of embarkation. His prose at this point echoes that of any tourist of the period, anxious not to miss the major monuments, eager to experience the sublime, the terrible, and the picturesque when crossing the Alps. He becomes increasingly engaged in specific observations as they cross the Atlantic, with spontaneous delight and pure description replacing the ear-

lier platitudes. He prides himself on his knowledge of Latin terminology for
the marine flora and fauna, as if to establish himself as a member of contemporary European intelligensia, keenly interested in natural science classification. His curiosity is wide-ranging and his verbal sketch of the storm at sea,
with its emphasis on displacement of objects animate and inanimate is dramatic and convincing.

He emerges as a wide-eyed and perspicacious observer of people as well
as things, however, only when he disembarks in the New World. One
imagines him, fifty-two years old and somewhat corpulent thanks to good
living, prancing about the streets of New York, Philadelphia, and points
in between, entranced by the Great New World he has discovered. His
astonishment at the motley architectural styles in New York is echoed by
de Tocqueville:

> When I first arrived in New York by that part of the Atlantic known as the
> East River, I was surprised to notice along the shore at some distance out
> from the city a number of little white marble palaces, some of them in clas-
> sical architectural style. The next day, when I looked more closely at one of
> those that had struck me most, I found that it was built of whitewashed
> brick and that the columns were of painted wood. All the buildings I had
> admired the day before were the same.[66]

At first in New York Mauro seems buoyed up by expectations of finding
wealthy patrons. This was, in fact, a period of accelerating prosperity with
speculators, "moneyed men," profiting from population growth and new
immigrant capital. But though such conspicuous investors as John Pintard
came to call, no solidly based patronage developed for Mauro. It may be that
he failed to provide the tame subjects of landscape and animal painting that
the budding bourgeoisie, often themselves with rural roots, dared indulge in.
Or, potential patrons may have been put off by Mauro's lack of deference. The
major groups of immigrants at this period were Scots, English, Irish,
and French, and the newly rich Americans, accustomed to meeting the few
Italian newcomers as laborers or shop-keepers, may have found Mauro
disconcerting.[67]

His observations on blacks, native people, women, fellow immigrants, and
petty crime in New York are unique for the period. Urban life is not his only
focus, however. He enjoys travelling by stagecoach, never complains of incon-
veniences, and marvels at the landscape and local agricultural customs. He has
a pleasant encounter with a "creole" (a term he defines as half Caucasian, half
American Indian). He flirts with her, then makes fun of himself: "At my age!"
Occasionally he will focus on a single day's adventure. The waterworks in

Philadelphia and the great reservoir on top of the hill (where now perches the Philadelphia Museum of Art) amaze him, and wandering in adjacent gardens he shows off his knowledge of Linnaean botanical terms and happily pockets some seeds to take home.

All is not idyllic, however. When Mauro seeks out examples of the Noble Savage, he finds that despite their handsome visages, they traded their furs for nails and whiskey. He applauds the little black chimney sweeps for their songs, but buys into the notion that negroes, especially the female variety, are unreliable and the Irish given to petty larceny. We glimpse the pathos of an Italian shoemaker who had expected instant prosperity in the New World. Penniless and claiming exploitation by the shopowner, he rants that had he arrived with the capital to set up his own home and shop, he would be doing to others as he had been done by.

Two threads, which are in a sense mutually incompatible, run through Mauro's assessment of the Americans. On the positive side, his high expectations for the workings of the new democracy are repeatedly confirmed. He watches the Fourth of July parade down by City Hall in New York and, ever sensitive to manifestations of liberty, fraternity, and equality, he is astonished at the absence of ceremonial uniforms or other indications of rank, only to be informed by a young friend that in America all public officials are considered equal. Even the policemen do not wear special uniforms. Americans are so honest that merchants can leave their goods untended on the street. They leave their doors unlocked (but he learned the hard way that one could not just wander in).

Mauro decided to strike out for the interior, leaving Teresa to look after herself in New York. He got only as far as Philadelphia, which seems to have riveted his attention. But it is at this point that he began to suspect a negative side to Utopia. He continued to find the Americans' forthright individualism wholly admirable. The principle of religious freedom, "when the independence of the country was acknowledged full toleration was enjoyed, with every man allowed to worship God according to the dictates of his own conscience,"[68] had his wholehearted support. He astutely observed, however, that universal tolerance, based as it was on the assumption that all opinions are equally valid, also allows each person to establish his own hierarchy of truth about the opinions of others. Ultimately this breeds a climate of judgmentalism, which he found offensive.

Mauro considered the Quakers remote and exclusive, and held them responsible for the puritanical attitudes he saw at every turn. He contended that, despite William Penn's insistence on freedom of belief, the Quakers tended toward bigotry which Mauro castigated not as immoral but worse, monotonous. At the same time, he admitted that there was much to admire about their customs: the artless straightforwardness of their meetings, their resistance to the whims of fashion, and their sober financial dealings which he contrasted with the spirit of speculation that ruled New York. But he sensed that they infected Philadelphia with a "moral tone that is too permeated by a mood of sobriety to please the generality of foreigners" – by which he no doubt meant himself – and found their prudishness antithetical to his own free-wheeling "sacred principle of independence". He also may have been sensing negative reactions that he himself, a foreigner with artistic pretensions and a mistress in tow, had unwittingly provoked.

Had he experienced rural Quakerdom, he might have been even more horrified. The Pennsylvania Quaker painter Edward Hicks confessed in his *Memoirs* that he "of course denounced everyone who sold or used distilled spirituous liquors" at the very time that Mauro was confessing that despite the challenge to find good wine, he managed to lay his hands on a couple of bottles a day for himself and his mistress. And worse, he might have discovered that painting was itself a suspect occupation. Hicks agonized over his calling as an artist, saying that painting itself "appears clearly to me to be one of those trifling, insignificant arts, which has never been of any substantial advantage to mankind . . . and in my view stands now enrolled among the premonitory symptoms of the rapid decline of the American Republic."[69] Mauro, on the contrary, was the product of a culture in which artists had for generations celebrated the benevolence of the state and the protective embrace of the Church through paintings.

Mauro's dissatisfactions often centered on local attitudes toward the human body, and he recognized that a profound fear of nudity lurked in the collective consciousness of this paradise on earth. The "Milady of a certain age" in the stagecoach to Trenton was horrified by the sight of boys swimming naked in a ditch, and averted her eyes.[70] The art establishment itself frowned on nakedness in art, as a scandal that erupted two years after Mauro's departure would show. John Vanderlyn was a young American artist whom Mauro mentioned several times and seems to have found particularly sympathetic. Vanderlyn had studied art in Paris for several years, and when he returned in 1815 he tried to exhibit his *chef d'oeuvre* at the Academy in New York. The painting showed a large and thoroughly nude Ariadne stretched out asleep on Naxos (fig. 16). The Academy refused to show it in their official opening exhibition on 25 October 1816 (where they had placed fig leaves on the statuary "as respect to public decorum"), on the grounds that it offended common decency.[71] It must have been hung earlier in the Academy as Mauro saw it there, and his wry account of the public reaction on the day he visited supports a

16   Asher B. Durand (after John Vanderlyn), *Ariadne Asleep on Naxos*, 1832, engraving.

modern author on the topic: "The voluptuous nude was enough to shock staid Americans of that generation despite the fact that it reflected the highest standards of the accepted classical taste of Napoleonic France."[72] An equally scandalous nude was the *Danae and the Golden Rain* by the Swedish artist Adolph-Ulric Wertmüller, an accomplished painter who had studied with Joseph-Marie Vien and arrived in Philadelphia in 1795, remaining there until his death in 1811. The *Danae*, like the *Ariadne*, was exhibited and provoked consternation, but large crowds as well.

When Mauro discovered, to his delight, that two of his prints were on exhibition at the Philadelphia Academy, he slyly commented that his engraving after his father's *St. Cecilia* (fig. 17) was more favourably looked upon than the one after Guido Reni's *Madonna and Child* "because it shows less nudity." He noted that the Academy did show some discreet female portraits, not an ounce of flesh showing unless they were of "French women and other foreigners." He was exultant, however, when one of the five gentlemen brought

17   Mauro Gandolfi (after Gaetano Gandolfi), *St. Cecilia Seated at the Organ*, before 1816, engraving.

around to his studio in New York by his friend Mr. Vecchio offered him $1,500 for his *Happy Dream*, a considerable sum in 1816. He refused to sell, and later joked about it with Teresa.

Mauro was inordinately proud of his *Dream*, a large and highly finished drawing with subtle tints of watercolor on vellum (fig. 18). Done in 1811, it made the entire voyage with Mauro. He referred to it later in his letters, and singled it out in his *testamento*.[73] It is easy to dismiss as bit of soft porn, but Mauro's fondness for it suggests that it had a deeper grounding in his creative imagination. Meticulously executed, it shows a woman exotically clothed and demurely posed, while others, conspicuously naked, float about provocatively

18   Mauro Gandolfi, *The Happy Dream*, 1811, brush and watercolor on vellum.

exhibiting their charms. It is difficult to place in any contemporary context, aside from being a *tour de force* as a study of female nudity. It may simply stand as Mauro's personal commentary on the prudery of the age which he held to be a permanent antagonist in his life as well as his art. Or it may suggest the existence of a silent market for exquisitely drawn eroticism. It has somehow survived despite its fragile medium. Mauro noted that after the visit by the Americans he was besieged with callers, some of whom were simply curious. One wonders if word of the *Dream* had got out.

His deeper concern was the effect that this flesh-phobia would have on the later development of art in America. At first it saddened him, and he wailed that it was a shame how the artists ignored the physical beauty that these healthy Americans flaunted. Then, after the stagecoach incident with the Milady, his concerns became more focused: "Alas! I said to myself, Painting will never find a good home here!" His recognized excellence as a practitioner of figurative art may explain his superior attitude toward the Philadelphia Academy of Art. His convictions, based on the centrality of the human figure in his own tradition and work, prompted him to berate the Keeper of the Philadelphia Academy, on the absence of figure study in his school. The growth of history painting would be stunted, he said, "so long as the puerile prejudice against studying the nude body" remained dominant. This was a powerful critique, as "history painting" (large scale figurative-narrative painting) was the apex of the European hierarchy of the fine arts.

Mauro's acerbic comments must be seen in context. Contrary to what he implied, teaching from nude models had passionate supporters among Philadelphia's artists who recognized it as an essential pillar of artistic instruction. They saw it as necessarily linked, for logistical reasons, to a training institution. In 1794 no less prestigious an artist than Charles Willson Peale had founded a short-lived art academy, the Columbianum, modelled on the Royal Academy in London. The classes in life drawing lasted only a month, and the school itself closed the following year. The Philadelphia Academy had been founded in 1805, as an association of stockholding members whose first objective was to generate revenue through public exhibitions. Local artists continued to press for the Academy to incorporate teaching facilities, and in 1810 formed themselves into an independent entity, the Society of Artists. The tribulations of establishing a permanent school with a viable teaching program was only one of the challenges that the Academy's founders faced. They were sophisticated enough to know that the emergence of a national school, devoutly to be desired, depended on cohesion within the artistic community that an academy would provide. Membership in such a respected institution would also validate the artist as a valuable member of urban society, a status still fragile in New World culture.

Two of Mauro's friends, Gideon Fairman and George Murray, along with the prominent painter Thomas Sully, belonged to a committee of the Society that drew up a plan in 1812 for a proposed art school in which students who had mastered the art of drawing from plaster casts would move on to drawing from the model, a standard academic sequence at the time. The plan was detailed, and included the selection and wages of the professors, student fees, and the hiring of a living model. In 1812 they even named a formal Professor of Anatomy. The following year the "first regular academy for studying the human figure," that is the life school, was announced but it closed in 1814, apparently from lack of interest.[74] A contributing reason may have been the costs for the model, heating, and lighting at the nighttime sessions.[75]

This most recent debacle on the teaching battlefield was fresh in everyone's mind in 1816, and Mauro must have known of it, but at the time it signified to him not only the aesthetic and spiritual impoverishment of American culture, but an affront to the Bolognese figurative tradition of which he was a proud exponent. On a visit to the Academy, Mauro admonished its keeper, Mr. Thackara, on the lack of figure study at the school.[76] He had no way of knowing that the issue would be resolved in 1820, when an enlightened curriculum was established. When Mr. Thackara proudly pointed out to him the painting *Elijah Resuscitating the Dead Man* by the up-and-coming Washington Allston, Mauro could not resist getting in a dig about its faulty figure drawing. He suggested that it would have been a "greater miracle to correct the distorted limbs of the resuscitated man than to bring him back to life." Public prejudice runs deep, however, and almost a century later Thomas Eakins staged his famous dispute over figure study with the authorities of the same institution, though by Eakins's time the argument had advanced beyond the question of nude versus no nude and centered instead on women's attendance at the life classes.

Mauro had hoped to find satisfactory work in the United States, and his tirades about the absence of figure training suggest that he might have accepted a professorship in this area at the Philadelphia Academy, had it been offered. It was exactly what he had taught at the Accademia Clementina, and the 1812 plan for the Academy had allowed for such a position and even one for a "professor of engraving." The teaching schedule was to be three two-hour sessions a week.[77] Whether he would have considered the salary of $400 per annum sufficient is not known. Another gainful employment for which Mauro was eminently qualified, but which he either disdained or was not invited to take, was making copies after old master paintings. An Academy document of 1805 states, as part of its educational objectives, "To promote the cultivation of the fine arts in America by introducing correct and elegant copies from works of the first Masters in Sculpture and Painting and by thus facilitating the access of such Standards."[78] "First Masters" were admittedly still in short supply, but the copies Mauro had produced in Europe, either as engravings or as precious objects on vellum, certainly obliged the requirements of "correct and elegant."[79]

Mauro's specialized field, that of the reproductive engraver, was the stock-in-trade of the professional printmaker before the invention of photography and the proliferation of photomechanical techniques after the mid-nineteenth century. Reproductive prints have been out of fashion on the art market for decades (though this trend may be in reverse), but it is necessary to see Mauro's accomplishments within the expectations of his times. Lithography, eminently suitable for reproducing the painted image and considerably cheaper to produce than engraving, began to gain a commercial foothold in the United States only in the 1820s. Although several of the printmakers Mauro mentioned as having met on his trip were experimenting with lithography, he seems never to have used the medium, possibly because both his painting and drawing styles were oriented toward precise lines and contours. Lithography seems also to have been tainted, in certain circles, with class implications whereby it was downgraded to a tool of the popular press, as distinct from the more labor-intensive engraving techniques. Cohn cites a description from an 1853 prospectus for reproductive engravings which she characterizes as "snob appeal": "They will be engraved for the most part in the LINE MANNER, which is the most costly and most generally admired style in Art, being five times more expensive than mezzotint, and fifty times greater than lithographs."[80]

Mauro was a virtuoso of both engraving and etching (fig. 19). These are known as the intaglio techniques, in which the print is taken from ink rubbed into lines incised in a copper plate, the surface of the plate having been wiped clean. An engraving is produced by the artist cutting the lines into the plate with a sharp pointed chisel called a burin. An etching results from the lines eaten into the plate by the action of acid. Through his Parisian training Mauro had gained control of the recalcitrant burin, which could be manipulated to suggest lights and darks by way of tapering lines interspersed with dots. We know that he had built up a considerable body of work by the time of his trip, as he mentioned bringing a case of engravings through Customs in New York. His pride in his skill increased further when he came to know the American engravers, whose command of the medium rarely equalled and never surpassed his own, and the hint of arrogance one senses in his appraisals of the American printmaking milieu must have stemmed from this realization. We know that he was offered commissions, and that his reputation had preceded him. The fact that he refused them is another matter.

19   Detail of fig. 23.

At that time, the most accomplished engravers in the United States had been trained in Europe, as there were no functioning teaching centers in the United States for a craft that was in any case best transmitted from master to apprentice. In New York Mauro both lived and worked briefly with Thomas Gimbrede, also trained in France, who produced high-quality portrait engravings of prominent public figures. He tells us that Gimbrede had engaged him to help with his current work-in-progress, the engraved portrait of Andrew Jackson (fig. 20). Collaboration on the production of a plate was common, and an analysis of this print helps us understand their relative contributions. Gimbrede would probably have reserved for himself the fine modelling of the face and possibly the hair (always a prominent decorative feature of official portraiture). It is tempting to posit Mauro's design contribution to the whimsical depiction of the marginal swamp complete with alligators, a fitting iconography for the General of the Battle of New Orleans in 1812. Such marginalia are almost non-existent in contemporary American engraved portraits. Mauro's fascination with natural-history whimsy is seen in a drawing he had prepared for an illustrated publication by the Botanical Gardens in Bologna His portrait of Antony van Leeuwenhoek (fig. 21)[81] presents the pioneer of microscopic zoological investigation surrounded by grotesquely magnified fleas. The motif of tailed women is repeated from the gilded figures on the Caprara carriage.

Given his gifts as a draughtsman and as an engraver, it is surprising that Mauro never moved into the profitable niche of portrait engraving which certainly existed and at which he excelled. He often spoke of his portraits with pride in his letters to Sedazzi, especially the one of his friend and fellow artist Pelagio Palagi (fig. 22).[82] Aside from Thomas Gimbrede's thriving trade in this area, Mauro's friends Archibald Robertson and William Leney both made profitable livings from portrait engravings, the latter having learned the stipple technique in England. In Philadelphia Charles Willson Peale under-

20   Thomas Gimbrede and Mauro Gandolfi (after Wheeler), *Major General Andrew Jackson of the United States Army*, 1816, engraving with etching.

stood the financial rewards implicit in the sales of multiple images of famous faces. In 1780 he advertised a subscription to the mezzotint portrait he had done after his painting of Benjamin Franklin.[83] Success in portraiture is a delicate thing, entailing such disparate skills as psychological insight and flattery. Mauro, with his faulty English and "sacred principle of independence," may simply have been unable to establish the essential entry points into the society that mattered, foreshadowing Samuel Palmer's experience some twenty years later in Rome. He also presented himself as a printmaker, not a painter, and aside from the few *peintres-graveurs* (such as Peale), the printmaker's

21 Mauro Gandolfi, *Portrait of Anton van Leeuwenhoek*, date
unknown, pen, black and brown ink, brown and gray wash.

status as artisan in the social hierarchy was rather below that of cultivated
gentleman or favored portraitist.

Mauro's failure to find a solution that could have freed him from his peren-
nial financial worries probably proceeded from several factors. The opportu-
nities for practicing engraving as a trade in the early nineteenth century were
indeed narrow and primarily limited to textual illustration which at this point
was still rare and costly. Etching (at which Mauro was also proficient) would
not be revived as a creative medium for another fifty years. The difficulty of
earning a living wage was exacerbated in America by an undeveloped distrib-

22　Mauro Gandolfi, *Portrait of Pelagio Palagi*, c.1820, oil on canvas.

ution system for the printed image. The absence of training facilities and the scarcity of tools also inhibited the development of a professional class with standards equivalent to those of Europeans.

Mauro's own agenda gave prominence to highly polished reproductive engravings of subjects that he considered culturally and politically correct, but which may have been incompatible with the market he faced. He found that demands for figurative representation were reduced to allegories of wealth, abundance, and transportation, or moralistic narratives. He was offered, and refused, employment by the "most renowned printmakers of the Philadelphia establishment, Fairman, Murray, Draper," which indeed they were. From 1810 to 1870 this firm produced not only book illustrations but most of the engraved banknotes in the United States which is exactly why Mauro ignored their advances. The chagrin he voiced in his "Voyage" stemmed from his feeling that "vignettes, allegories, invoices and the smallest copper plates to use in their Bible, or some little portrait" would not fully utilize his skills. He scorned commissions for the "Quaker Bible" and bills of sale, and though the illustrative demands of the American Protestants may well have offended his anti-clericalism, he was quite willing, both before and after his trip, to engrave religious paintings for the *Musée Français*, probably because the originals were by the great Baroque artists he had been trained to revere. Also, once repatriated he happily produced decorative vignettes. Still, when faced with the opportunity to contribute to a project that represented an iconic moment in the American democracy intended to stimulate patriotic pride, he balked.

John Trumbull, the American painter *par excellence* of historical subjects, offered Mauro the long-term and highly lucrative project of engraving his *Signing of the Declaration of Independence*. The idea of painting dramatic scenes from the American revolution was Benjamin West's, and by November 1784 Trumbull had begun to work on a series that would commemorate major events of the War of Independence, apparently with the approval of his friend Thomas Jefferson. The subjects he chose were the *Declaration of Independence*, the *Surrender of Lord Cornwallis at Yorktown*, the *Surrender of General Burgoyne at Saratoga*, and the *Resignation of Washington*. After various journeys back and forth to Europe he had returned in September 1815 to New York which by then had assumed the status of a cultural center.

In May 1816 Trumbull acquired a new house on Hudson Square, intending to finish individual portraits of the notable personnages signing the *Declaration*. It was probably in the early summer of that year that he approached Mauro with the proposal of engraving the painting. He would have had, at that time, only the oil sketches to show his prospective engraver. In December he travelled to Baltimore with oil sketches of his ambitious series of four paintings, hoping in vain to secure backing to enable him to work them up into full scale canvases. He moved on to Washington and this time was successful with his proposal to execute the paintings for the rotunda of the Capitol. The contract was signed on 15 March 1817 for $8,000 for each painting and they were finally installed in 1826.

The story of Trumbull's laborious attempts to find an engraver for the *Declaration*, a landmark of American painting, is well documented and tells us a great deal about the world of reproductive engraving in the United States into which Mauro ultimately chose not to enter. Trumbull planned from the start to utilize the project as a commercial enterprise, as was customary at the time, by selling engravings of the paintings by subscription. He well knew that the profits he hoped to reap depended heavily on his choice of engraver, but he was worried about the production costs, estimating "the cost of the enterprise to be at least $10,000."[84] He records that "I engaged the elder Mr. Heath, the first engraver living, to engrave the plate, for which I have engaged to pay him $7,000, but expect the cost to be 50 percent more," and then "No less than $10,000 must be expended on this object, before a dollar can be recovered in return." He notes that the fee he is offering for the engraving is the same as Mr. Heath had been offered to engrave Benjamin West's *Death of Nelson*.[85] All this suggests that Mauro was bragging when he claimed that Trumbull offered him $20,000.

The next development is signalled by a remark Trumbull made to a friend in London, Andrew Robertson, on 28 June 1816: "Mr. Heath the Father is dead. Is this true? He had agreed unconditionally to engrave my picture of the *Declaration of Independence* and the picture is very nearly finished. I am now in treaty with an Italian engraver who lately arrived here and brings highly respectable evidence of his talent. But it will be highly vexatious if I should find the report false, having put my work into inferior hands."[86] Trumbull is surely referring to Mauro here, though not by name. The dates are perfectly in accord. The standards he set exceeded mere craftsmanship. He asks Robertson to look into two English engravers for him, but injects a warning note: "and give me the moral as well as the professional characters of these gentlemen. I am not so sanguine as many are on subjects of this sort."[87] One can imagine Mauro snorting at what he would consider puritanical sentiments.

By February 1818 Trumbull had begun to send out letters drumming up subscriptions for the engraving which he hoped would offset the costs of its production. The potential subscriber was meant to be seduced by Trumbull's historical exactitude, his price, and the opportunity to decorate one's home with a patriotic statement. He proudly describes the painting with the kind of precise historical detail that drove Mauro to distraction: "The dresses are faithfully copied from the costume of the time, the present fashion of pantaloons and trousers being then unknown among gentlemen."[88] And further, "The print will contain forty-seven portraits of the most eminent men, some of them whole lengths, and will be so executed in the finest state by the first engraver of the age, so as to form within the frame an elegant monumental piece of furniture, at the average price of 42½ cents a head."[89] Mauro, who had seen only the oil sketch, had been dismayed by a mere twenty-eight portraits. The crowd had swelled by 1818, and Trumbull gave a frank explanation: the prints would be priced by the number of heads.

At any rate, the commission's demands for journalistic exactitude struck Mauro as tedious: "So many portraits, so many boots, shoes, cravats, and twenty-six costumes in the French mode, I concluded that I would undoubtedly die of boredom before I could finish it . . . [and] so I refused this commission, as honorable in subject as it was maladapted to an artist nourished in the Italian school." Mauro thus rejected a unique opportunity to make American art history.

The challenge was eventually taken up in 1820 by the young Asher B. Durand. The engraving was exhibited at the New York Academy in 1824 and established Durand's reputation. His technique is competent but less refined than Mauro's.[90]

Mauro's final days in New York reflected his growing cynicism as his vision of a brave New World tarnished rapidly. An evening at the theater made him homesick for his Teatro Comunale in Bologna, a charming creation of Antonio Bibiena. Musical performances were grotesque at best. There was no reason to remain any longer. The account of his journey back across the Atlantic is anticlimactic, though there are amusing stories and a blood-curdling adventure. It occasioned, however, one peculiar series of events. Mauro described how, when he had made up his mind to return, a young man named William Main begged to accompany him on the return voyage, to remain with him in Italy as an apprentice engraver. The deal seems to have been clinched when, through Main's family connections, a contract was agreed whereby Mauro and Teresa would have their way paid back to Italy with a stop-off in Gibraltar included. Main's short biographies contain the rudiments of this story, and add a bemused comment that soon after reaching Florence he was shocked to find that Mauro had inexplicably disappeared. In fact, Mauro remained in Florence until 1818, producing engravings for the firm of Luigi Bardi. Main stayed on as well, studying with the engraver Van

Morghern before returning to New York for a respectable career as a print-maker there. Is it possible that Mauro got his free trip home, then reneged on his bargain to take Main on as a pupil? Was he really the scoundrel that many had accused him of being?

By May 1818 Mauro had established residence in Milan, where he produced reproductive engravings for the prominent publishing firm of Pietro and Giuseppe Vallardi, some of which are dated to 1825 or 1826. His life there can be pieced together from Scarabelli's anecdotal account and from the forty-seven unpublished letters dating from 24 April 1818 to 19 June 1822 that he wrote from Milan to Luigi Sedazzi.[91] These letters offer a picture of Mauro's personality that echoes the one we glimpse in the "Voyage." He shows himself confidentially to a friend as genial and affectionate but also vain and acrimonius, often enraged at real or perceived injustices. He describes some lucrative gem-dealing, begun in New York (in which Sedazzi was apparently complicit), as well as an active trade in his own engravings with prominent German dealers.

Mauro's work consisted not only of reproductive engravings but also of finished drawings and watercolours, often on vellum, for a specialized if somewhat precious market in fine copies of old masters. His penchant for quirky iconography remained. In a letter to Sedazzi, which chides his friend for having termed his prints "stampuccie" ("lousy little prints"), he sends a proof impression of his *Amor dormiente* (*Love Sleeping*) (fig. 23),[92] a pendant to his engraving *Putto sulla croce* (*The Christ Child Sleeping on the Cross*). His finished engraving of *Love Sleeping*, in which the putto figure is the exact reverse of the Child on the Cross, bears a poetic inscription describing the insistent nature of sensual love, thus suggesting slyly that the Christ Child and an erotic putto are mirror images of one another, whether they dream of love or crucifixion.

In September 1819 Mauro moved again to a larger and quieter house with extra rooms for guests. He describes other commissions for reproductive engravings that he continued to make, including more for the *Musée Français* and one from Vienna, as well as sales of prints and drawings. Once more he apparently prospered.[93] His engravings must have been his main source of income, though he did not scorn less lucrative tasks and mentioned receiving "three zecchini" for one of his "figurine," apparently small decorative drawings.[94] He specified that one of these was meant to be applied to a little box, and in the list of all his works appended to his *testamento* he mentions "twenty-eight designs suitable for a "tabbacchiera," or snuff-box. Such objects have a short life span and even those that have survived are difficult to trace today. One of them appeared on the New York art market several years ago. Round, two inches in diameter, with a watercolored drawing of a young couple fixed to the lid, it was charming, elegant, and signed with his initials.[95] He claimed

23   Mauro Gandolfi, *Love Sleeping*, *c*,1820, engraving and etching.

to have done numerous *ritrattini*, or "little portraits," but doesn't mention the medium. Three portrait drawings in the Fondazione Cini in Venice bear his calligraphic monogram signature, "M.G."[96]

Mauro remained nostalgic about travel after his return. In a letter of 21 November 1819 to an old family friend Giorgio Fornasari he fantasized about making just one more trip. Commenting on the news that Fornasari had just travelled to a far corner of the Mediterranean, he dreamed that they should set forth together:

> Imagine how it would be if you decided to traverse the immense Ocean, and to live some months in America. Doing this would rejuvenate you, I assure you, and people who are able to do so would be wrong not to. Such people deserve to live in a stagnant lagoon with the oysters and the sea-sponges, and not on this earth. Because of one miserable woman and an unfair judgment, I expected to have died a criminal. One lovely voyage has compensated me for the loss of all my worldly goods, my honor vindicated and my independence recovered.

He concluded that since his friend is free and rich, they should aim first for Calcutta where they would trade precious stones, then pass Ceylon and over the seas to Arabia and the Euphrates, or first to Isfahan and then to Jerusalem and Cairo. Arriving at Constantinople, they would go on beyond the Black Sea and visit famous Georgia and the Circassians. Then on their return to Bologna, "in front of the fireplace, we will tell stories of the stupendous works of man and nature, and as for those spiteful dolts who shrug their shoulders and say it can't be done, well, their jaws will just hang open! But you'll object that you'd run the risk of death and I answer, no more nor less than lounging outside your front door. To avoid dangers, one needs only experience, caution, and being comfortably equipped with abilities and money."[97]

Mauro confided in Sedazzi. His comments on current work in progress show that his wit and vigour continued unabated. A new and hysterical tone, however, is increasingly evident in the letters throughout 1820 and 1821, with furious references to an anonymous item that had been published in the *Gazzetta Privilegiata di Bologna* on 17 January 1820 and reprinted in the *Gazzetta di Milano* shortly thereafter that had "forever changed my life for the worst."[98] This item seems at first reading innocuous enough, being simply a florid encomium dedicated to Mauro's son Democrito who had finally established himself as a sculptor. It goes on, however, with evident malice aforethought to say that Democrito was the son of the eminent engraver and painter Mauro, who formerly lived "in our city," but who seems to have "foresaken his family and now lives in Milan, where he is highly praised and amply rewarded for his noble efforts." Apparently our famous voyager had skipped out again on family support obligations and with his whereabouts being advertised, his cover was blown.

Caterina seized on the news and in August descended on Milan. She sought shelter with Mauro's friends and failing that appealed to him to take her in "as a servant confessing to have lost the title of wife." Mauro sent her home, saying she would do more damage as a servant than as a wife.[99]

The matter came to a head with yet another court case and this time Mauro was held accountable for lapsed payments to Caterina. He claimed that the scandal impugned him unfairly, and stated that his brothers and relatives had reproved him because of the dishonor brought upon him by that "impudent female." Even the faithful Protasio, who had been the godfather to Mauro's first son, Raffaele, was now his enemy.[100] One can not help but admire Caterina for her persistence.

The judge had originally decreed a legally enforced reunion "commanded by Mother Church to save my soul since I was living with another woman."[101] In November Mauro was able to write to Luigi, "The final sentence of the Tribune of Milan judges me guilty, she being called on to desist and deemed separated from her husband, and I to sacrifice 300 lire annually. This solely to clear my relatives of further dishonor from the infernal serpent."[102] The matter finally resolved, by December 1822 Mauro felt that he could now move back to his "patria," though not without some doubts.[103]

The house he built for himself in Bologna suggests that he was still a fairly wealthy man. A posthumous description of via Riva Reno #41 by the nineteenth-century chronicler of the city's streets Giuseppe Guidicini reads, "Built by the celebrated engraver Mauro, son of Gaetano Gandolfi in 1826." It was a house designed by Mauro himself to accommodate his needs as an artist.[104] The Reno, by whose banks the house stood, was one of the many canals in Bologna. It was later paved and made into a wide street that was obliterated by the Allied bombing of 1944, so no trace remains of the house. In 1828 Mauro was secure enough financially to order a Bohm pianoforte to be sent up from Rome for his daughter, Clementina.[105]

He remained on good terms with his son who, writing his autobiography in the third person, was proud to say that he himself "had a studio in Milan generously endowed with commissions from private gentlemen as well as from various municipalities for works in marble . . . modelling portraits in ivory paste in a style that was fairly new and finding thereby great favor among the Milanese, and in only two years received 217 commissions, receiving rich compensations."[106] Faithful to the end, though something of a caricature of his father, Democrito boasted of having inherited Mauro's revolutionary fervor, and claimed in his memoirs that the first words he heard as a newborn, uttered by his father, were "Evviva Bonaparte!"[107] He revered Napoleon's memory long after the Emperor's fall, working for a time in Vienna, but a large marble portrait statue of Metternich he presented there, "in classical style, when he was young," resembled Napoleon I too closely so he fell from favor and returned to Milan in 1827.[108] It is told that he went around Milan wearing a monocle to demonstrate his independence, but soon everybody was doing it. He continued in Milan to make objects of ivory paste to commemorate Napoleon, and died there in 1874 in the "Institute for Aged Septugenarians" where he had lived for seven years.

Mauro's mistress, Teresa Diani, had remained with him throughout his peregrinations.[109] He rewarded her fidelity in 1827 by registering her as owner of the house on via Riva Reno, possibly to circumvent the efforts of Caterina to stake a claim. Once in legal possession, Teresa proceeded to leave him for another man, one Gaetano Tommasi, and took the ownership of the house with her. Helpless to retaliate, and evicted from what was now Teresa's property, Mauro moved to what he termed "the attic" of the Palazzo Bentivoglio, once the site of both his and his father's studios. He addressed an appeal for financial support to the Commission of Veterans' Administration in Bologna in 1832, portraying himself as old, sick, and indigent.[110] We do not know if this stipend was granted, but the pitiful listing of his worldly goods in his *testamento* of 1833 indicates that he was, in fact, impoverished. He died of typhoid fever on 4 January 1834 in Bologna.

Mauro's experiences in the New World reflect the image of a young culture straining towards its identity as viewed by a sharp-witted, if somewhat dour, Italian. His biases, as well as his hopes for a better life in the United States, are clear. His observations reflect the conflict between his idealistic expectations and his encounters with the American reality: unabashed enthusiasm alternating with repulsion, although we can also imagine him viewed by his colleagues as arrogant, opinionated, and full of foreign affectations, since he so overtly despised the art produced by these new Americans. We experience with him the culture shock felt by a critical European visitor at a sensitive point in history. In the end he failed to accept the American way of life just as the Americans failed to accept him. It is possible that the xenophobia that would assume conspicuous proportions with the influx of immigrants into the United States in the 1840s was already becoming evident. A few contemporary accounts by other professional foreign visitors support this hypothesis, though there are conspicuous exceptions such as the colorful Lorenzo da Ponte – also with an amorous past – who had been Mozart's Italian librettist and who succeeded mightily.[111] There are shadowy hints in Mauro's text, however, at a prejudice, on the part of the worthy egalitarian Americans, against a sophisticated and probably supercilious Italian.[112]

Democrito sculpted the marble portrait bust of Gaetano that adorns the tombstone marking the grave in the Certosa that Mauro improbably shares with his father, with whom he apparently never made peace. According to Scarabelli, its florid inscription is intended to vindicate Mauro *in aeternitatem*, to have the last word with Caterina as it were. "These words are meant to honor his memory, celebrated for his art, and to settle the account with posterity of the torments he suffered from the perfidy of those close to him, and embittered always by the betrayal of the good and of his native land." Scarabelli concluded his encomium, written nine years after Mauro's death, with the assertion that "in life the artist had suffered tribulations due to the treachery of false friends, was ever sensitive to the misfortunes that befell good men and his native land, but that the most sympathetic are often the least happy."[113] He mused about Mauro's character, describing him as being

as irascible as he was affectionate. Many afflictions tried the strength of his soul, and however benevolent he was, he never had peace on this earth. Education taught him a patience which does not falter when faced by the vicissitudes of evil fortune. He felt that men were more endowed with vices than virtues: Dissatisfied with the social institutions of his day, powerless to change them, envied and tormented not only by his emulators but by the disloyal and lesser men, he sought tranquillity in many places, but never found it.[114]

The "Viaggio" recounts one of Mauro's attempts, perennially doomed to failure, to resolve his life by a radical change of place.

Voyage to the United States of America in 1816

undertaken and described by Mauro Gandolfi,

celebrated painter and engraver.

Copy of the Original Manuscript
annotated by Michelangelo Gualandi
Bologna, 1834

Voyage to the United States of America

Undertaken by Mauro Gandolfi in the year 1816[1]

REASONS FOR MY VOYAGE TO AMERICA

Dearest Friend

The reasons for my Voyage to America are as follows. Man, as you know, is susceptible to two impulses: the instinct with which he is born, and reason. It is certain that, finding himself in adverse circumstances, a man who remains faithful to his nature will in spite of the habits acquired through good breeding, favor instinct over reason, reason being in any case only a cold calculation of his own self interest, or his disadvantage. Consider, for instance, a man faithful to the principles of honesty but united in his second marriage to a female whose apparent moral qualities fill him with happiness. Later she sheds her mask and associates herself with other hypocritical villains like herself, who abet her in murdering the honor of her husband as well as stealing his health and his possessions. He begins to feel a profound aversion to the vain considerations of reason, and abandons himself entirely to instinct. Herein, my friend, lies the powerful motivation that, on 6 February 1816, prompted me to sacrifice my worldly possessions (with no more thought of them, if I may say so, than the laborious and placid beaver). May the perfidious harpies and my other depraved persecutors not go unpunished.

Though only a scanty portion remained of the fruits of my many years of honest toil, I resolved to restore my wounded soul by visiting the ever felicitous United States of America. And if inevitable fate should dictate that I lose at once my friends and

Page 46   Detail of fig. 34.

Facing page   Detail of fig. 41.

the practical advantages of my life, then I would at least be partly consoled by fulfilling a project that is not given to every man
to realize. It has been proved elsewhere that the best remedy for
the sickness of the soul is travel, and if the remedy should be
proportionate to the sorrow, then mine would not be a short
journey. Indeed between the outbound journey and the return,
my voyage turned out to be about nine thousand and nine hundred miles. Nature has a way of healing the wounds of the spirit, as it heals those of the body. This is exactly what happened to
me, though I went through an incredible sequence of inconve-
niences and dangers, including that of death itself. Not only did
these seem light compared with the injuries and affronts that I
had already suffered, but in fact the delightful experience of travelling comfortably had such a healing effect on my soul that I
soon forgot my past grievances, and I felt as though I had been
reborn to a new and pleasurable life.

Trip from Bologna to Bordeaux

I decided, then, not to board a ship at a Mediterranean port,
as many Italians do, but rather at an Atlantic port. One reason
for this was that the Gulf of Lyon is stormy, and the proximity
of Sardinia and Corsica also are the source of sea storms, but the
strongest reason (would you believe it?) is that the great sea current that originates in the Gulf of Mexico passes through the
Straits of Gibraltar and when it enters the Mediterranean, it
usually brings with it a contrary wind, making it as difficult to
exit as it was easy to enter. It caused me no little relief, on arriving in Milan from Bologna, to learn that a certain woman who
was obligated neither by family relationship nor oath of fidelity
to me, nevertheless made it clear to me that I should not venture
alone, exposed to so many dangers on land and on sea. Despite
my lively protestations she chose to share with me the good
times and the bad. We planned that she would remain in New
York and enjoy the urban pleasures thereof while I travelled
through the United States.

We then found ourselves in Turin, a city of fine architecture.
We arose in the morning to contemplate the Savoy Alps, whose
imposing peaks were hidden among the clouds. Sometimes
when the traveller finds himself just beneath them they no

longer look like clouds but rather a vast liquid sea that blinds the eye and which, reflecting the shimmering rainbow of the sun, appears as the living image of the blessed residence of the Gods. From this delightful illusion one reverts to the sweetest melancholy, crossing the sombre valleys and the narrow paths whose darkness seems no less than the very sleep of nature herself. Then one hears a murmur that grows louder as one approaches a smiling and picturesque scene: a torrent of water plunges precipitously from above over steep rocks, then descends to the plain, where it resumes its placid and tranquil course. There are a thousand other wondrous things which, for the sake of brevity, I shall omit.

Leaving behind the extravagancies of nature, we arrived in Lyon, a beautiful city and a rich one thanks to its impressive factories. The Rhône consoled and restored us after the laborious passage through the Alps, and transported us cheaply with our baggage to Avignon, once the residence of the Roman Popes. From there by carriage we reached Nîmes, a city which contains some ancient Roman monuments worthy of a foreigner's admiration. There is the amphitheatre and above all the famous temple called the Maison Carrée, whose perfect architectural style with its wealth of ornamentation and its pristine condition remains unequalled to this day in all of Rome. We then proceeded to Montpellier, famous for its university, its industries, and gardens. The so called Peyrou is without a doubt the most beautiful architectural monument decorating any of the delightful public avenues in Europe.[2] In my opinion this city is enough in itself to make the South of France so fascinating. From Montpellier, passing through Bézier, we travelled on the famous Canal of Languedoc, a marvellous waterway built to establish commercial ties between the Mediterranean and the Ocean. Hence we arrived in Toulouse, where the remains of some ancient Roman buildings are still visible. We resumed transportation by water on the Garonne river, which leads to the sumptuous city of Bordeaux, among the most active sea ports in the World. Having arrived here on 28 March of the year 1816, we took comfortable lodgings to enjoy a little rest, and then visited the magnificent Bourse, the great theatre, the Cathedral, and the Square.

I wandered through the extensive dock area, crowded with ships of every nation, looking to discover the most comfortable and the safest way to travel by sea. As a result of my investigations, I chose an American merchant vessel, because the crew seemed trustworthy and because the rooms, being very clean, would be healthy. However, before I signed a contract, I once again entreated my good travelling companion to consider returning home instead of exposing herself to the discomforts and perils of a long sea journey, but my solicitude was in vain. Fearless and loyal, she did not want to abandon me, and after assigning all her worldly goods by way of an autograph testament to her sisters in the first instance, and to my daughter Clementina in the second, she blithely resigned herself to her fate with me.

After I had contacted the ship brokers Lafitte, Cerisi & Co., I made an agreement with Captain Almy. Here, to my confusion as a cultivated European, I had my first lesson in the honesty of the free Americans. I had requested a receipt for the sum of money that I had paid out and for our possessions that we had entrusted to them. The Captain and the Cargo Officers assembled there burst out laughing, telling me that this was an unnecessary formality. I remarked that my suggestion was not made with the intention of offending them, but was only a precaution in case we should be forcibly separated from our belongings during the journey. I thought that a note written by the Captain might prove useful. He agreed, and I was satisfied as follows:

"Rec.d from Mr. Moro Gandolfi the sum of one thousand six hundred francs for the amount of his passage and his lady's and their effects on board the brigadier William Henry bound for New York, and to arrange provision for them at my table. These effects consist of three trunks of wearing apparel, one case of engravings, and several small articles."

Bordeaux 5 April 1816

Peter Almy

24 Anne-Marguérite-Henriette Rouillé de Marigny, Baroness Hyde de Neuville, *The Family of Baron Hyde de Neuville in Their Ship's Cabin*, June 1816, watercolor.

A first-class transatlantic ship's cabin at the time of Mauro's journey.

PASSPORT

On 11 April I obtained my passport, though there was some difficulty on the part of Prefect Dumont, who was trying to prevent massive French immigration into the United States.[3] I obtained it by claiming the hallowed rights of the people and handing over some money. We took possession of two cabins in the Captain's quarters. We dined at his table and were treated very well. We had also, by good fortune, met there the Subcaptain, or Supercargo, and some families, all most courteous.[4] Only we two shared these lodgings with them as the other passengers stayed below deck, to spend less but to suffer more in the end. At last we were launched onto the salty main, to challenge the immense ocean with all our physical strength. In thirty-five days (according to the Gazette of New York), with a mixture of pleasures completely new to us and well-founded fears of death, we reached America.

SHIP

Dearest friend, quite a different pen from mine would be needed to convey realistically the multiple things that can be seen and heard on a journey such as this. The ship was like a great floating castle, inhabited by people of different nations as well as quadrupeds and birds. Many trades were practiced there, everything needed for human life could be found. One could be pleasantly entertained by music or reading, or learn other languages, customs, and traditions. A castle, I said, but one that draws its security from the sea, that very element which is often the source of its own destruction. The very fact of the ship's existence attests to man's power, his pride, and his extreme greed.

PRODUCTS OF THE SEA   And then there were the odd atmospheric phenomena, and the many and varied labours of the crew, all obedient to the will of their absolute Master, the Captain. The sight of innumerable species of fishes, birds, and plants, as well as the encounters with other ships in the distance flying a friendly flag. All these dissipated the boredom and the monotony of the sea. Among the most bizarre products of the sea, I'd like to mention here some vegetal ones which, clustered together, form large floating meadows quite refreshing to the eye of the observer.[6] Thanks to the kindness of the Pilot, I frequently had the chance to get my hands on some of these plants to examine them. One day I saw one that excited my curiosity more than any other. After laying it on the deck, I found that it measured twenty-two Bolognese feet. It was a tube, or rather a stem with feet. It was in the shape of a whip and with only one wavy leaf. The rest consisted of a pale jelly-like substance of a blond hue like amber. It is called *Kelpe*. It resembles somewhat the *bamboo* of the southern sea (*fucus bucinalis*).[7] So often did I regret that I had not brought with me vials and alcohol to preserve these strange objects. Schools of dolphins frolicked, leaping out of the waves, chasing one another, and every so often spraying high jets of water. Twice we saw a whale, thankfully only from afar, still as a sleeping rock. With the help of a telescope I was able to examine that voluminous monster. The sea lions, the seals, the dangerous sawfish, and the sharks were wounded several times by a harpoon tied to a long iron chain, thrown by the vigorous arm of our Captain. Among the molluscs the most attractive is certainly the so-called "Portuguese man o'war" (*molusca holeturia fisicalis*). It perfectly resembles a fluted cup of purest crystal, in the middle of which lives the tiny creature, who swims using some colourful peduncles situated underneath its body.

Storm at Sea

Alas! Amidst so many pleasures we were not spared the wrath of the sea and the heavens. A bitter north-west wind and a ferocious storm poured over us and threw us up violently into the the Bay of Biscay. Then an even more vicious tempest drove us back, and after a few days we were on the high seas of the Azores. We then endured to a rainstorm preceded by a thick fog, which, however, didn't turn out to be a total disaster as by way of sheets attached by their corners and suspended in mid-air, forming a concave shell, we were to our great satisfaction able to collect plenty of fresh water.

But although Almy was extremely good to us, he nevertheless had to satisfy his whims. Frantic to fish, he decided to approach the banks of Newfoundland, which in turn treated us to a wild storm that lasted almost three days and three nights, exhausting both our strength and our hope. The sails were hauled down with great difficulty, the skiff, suspended off the stern, was shattered in a thousand pieces. The doors of the rear deck were closed hermetically, and the wretched passengers were, in a manner of speaking, buried alive. One of the spars snapped off, and everything was upside down, in frightful disorder. The sailors could do nothing but continue to work the pumps in order to empty the water that was pouring in. The ship was abandoned to the mercy of the winds and the waves, like huge mountains of frothing water, clashed and retreated in turn as if to engulf us and swallow us down into their black and fetid maw. In fact, everything was foretelling our demise, and even the Captain himself stepped down into our cabin with the paleness of death on his face. I should note that the cabins were always lit, either by sunlight coming through the glass window of the so-called "Dome," or by way of a lamp fixed to a pivot and burning throughout the night. The insistent rolling and constant shaking in all directions tormented my companion and me intolerably while we were lying in bed, although neither of us suffered from seasickness. But never did we lose heart.

Sea Becalmed

Towards the end of the third day the winds dropped, followed by a perfect calm. When we threw out the sounding line, we realized that we had passed the southern tip of Newfoundland's

sand bank, between 42 and 43 degrees of northern latitude.[7] The
Captain had the major damage repaired, then went back to fishing for huge turtles off the lifeboat.[8] The good wines brought
from Bordeaux restored us so that we felt as though reborn to a
new life.

ICEBERGS   However, here we chanced upon another serious danger: the
masses of ice that drift out of the Canadian St. Laurence river.
These, floating and scattered here and there, cause great damage
to the ships that collide with them.

LAND IS SIGHTED   Everyone longed to catch sight of land. When, from the
crow's nest the look-out shouted "land ho, gentlemen!",[9] he was
echoed by a universal cry of joy, and I cannot describe to you the
exhilaration that pervaded my senses. The sounding line indeed
showed us signs of the yellowish earth of the American coast,
and after midnight of that happy day one of the pilots from the
port came to lead us safely ashore. He continued to take sound-
ings of the seabed, each time announcing the measurements of
its depth aloud, with a pleasant sing-song tune of three notes.
And oh, what a marvellous surprise it was when at daybreak I
clambered up onto the deck, and saw before my very eyes the
port and the city of New York.

CITY OF NEW YORK   I have never seen a panorama comparable with this for bizarre
and picturesque effect. Since, as you well know, people of differ-

25 (*facing page*) Baron Axel Leonhard Klinckowström, *Harbor and Docks of New York from Brooklyn on Long Island*, 1824, aquatint.

The New York harbor was active with both steam- and wind-powered water-craft at this time.

26 John Hill (after William Guy Wall), *Manhattan from Brooklyn Heights*, 1823, aquatint.

A view across the harbor with the New York skyline and the New Jersey hills beyond.

VISITORS TO THE SHIP

ent nationalities have from the very beginning collaborated in building it, its architectural styles vary widely. The cultivated traveller will find here an inventory, so to speak, of all the styles, fashions, and forms that can be seen throughout the world. What renders the effect so piquant and curious is to see a humble hut alongside a palace, a peristyle imitating the Pantheon right next door to an ugly wooden house. Each proprietor strives to outdo the other in painting the exterior of his house, resulting in an effect of great charm. Now one sees a cornice below the roof, then another one crenellated in pyramid form as in Flanders, now another terraced in the Asian style, or one crowned with copper.[10]

Three officials entered our ship, as was customary: the doctor, the customs house representative, and the reporter. The first compiled his medical report. The third took note of those people on the ship interested in the merchandise it contained, and recorded the names of the passengers according to the details they chose to give, including their professions if they liked to make this known. As for me, I demurred (and not without good reason), allowing him to note down only my first name which sounded like 'Moro' (from Mauro) and Teresa *Wife of Moro*. This is how it was published in the merchant chronicle *Advertiser*, and I cherish the name if for no other reason than to confound

27   John Joseph
Holland, *Broad Street
looking toward Old
Federal Hall, with Dutch
Gabled Houses*, 1797,
watercolor.

New York's miscellany of
architectural styles
included Federal, Greek
Revival, Dutch gabled,
and plain domestic.

CUSTOMS PROCEDURE

some Bolognese slanderer, someone who would sully other people's reputations.

Curiously, the customs officials seem to have been chosen from among their peers for their gentle tempers and polite manners. One could almost interpret their performance as the frontispiece of the great book of trust and discretion that characterizes this regenerate nation. The official asked me whether I carried anything of commercial value in my trunks. I told him I didn't, and that I had only one case of that nature which contained *paper engravings*, a professional tool. He then told me to take all my trunks off the ship except for that one, and to proceed to the Customs House in Wall Street to declare their value, which I did.[11] I entered a large room, in the middle of which the Chief Officer was sitting on a little stool, receiving the declarations. I undervalued my possessions, still not knowing what was going to happen to my engravings. He made me put my hand on the Bible, then taxed me eleven dollars for a capital value that in Europe would have been six dollars, but in America became twenty-five or thirty. I returned to the ship with my receipt, and my case was then released to me. Take note: nobody inspected it.

The same practice applies to merchandise of intrinsic value such as watches, silver, or jewellery and the like. Amazed by such magnanimity on the part of the Government (as must be anyone who has travelled in Italy), I began to interrogate these good Americans on the issue of trust. They told me that they were well aware of losing several million dollars in customs revenue each year, but that they tolerated such a loss rather than to foment bad faith and suspicion, especially since the damage was not borne by one Prince or King but was distributed impartially over one hundred and twenty thousand citizens, whose intrepid hearts and stout arms would stand in good stead for the lost money when, in defending their liberty against its enemies, the enemies themselves would have to bear the costs.

I wish, however, to disclose a small incident, so that you may understand how primitive the fine arts still were in this country in 1816. I had, among the things I unloaded from the ship, my indispensible manikin.[12] The Customs Officer was evidently curious about this, and mistook it for some kind of automated puppet which I intended to use for profit. It was no good my explaining to him otherwise, as he insisted that he knew very well about models of flesh and blood, but that painters didn't use wooden models, and that I had to take it to the Customs House. I perforce had to obey, and had it carried over to the office, laughing at the ignorance of this official. But to my astonishment his ignorance was shared by his countrymen. Not only did his fellow officials assure me that they were unfamiliar with such a thing (though they accepted my protesations) but even the people in the street when they saw it rushed up and crowded around, most curious about this great novelty. The boys in particular were crying "A black man! A little wooden black man!".[13]

FREEDOM OF LIFE IN THE
UNITED STATES

Before, however, I venture to give you a sketch of this beautiful country, I have to tell you that nobody asks you to show your passport, nobody tries to find out who you are or what you want to do.[14] No one is required to carry an identity card, and once one has set foot in this land, one is free to travel across the whole of the United States, and to carry out one's business exempt from any inspection, contribution, or customs tax. Every class of people is accepted, and one would say that justice, security of person, and of property, in short all virtues are born and bred here, and that vices have disappeared from this fortunate land. Oh God! I exclaimed to myself, comparing this with other countries. Could it be that mankind poisons its own kind, seeing itself constantly thwarted by so many humiliating laws? Is it the laws that create the customs, or rather do ordinary customs of morality create the laws? You be the judge: these phenomena seem truly inexplicable to me.

PRESIDENCY OF THE UNITED STATES

These sixteen immense families, or rather Republics, united according to the common principles of liberty and equality, occupy the most pleasant part of North America, from 31 (nowadays from 26) to 49 degrees of latitude, and from 69 to 109 of longitude.[15] Their heroic forefathers threw off the brutal yoke of their mother country in 1783,[16] and in 1816 they numbered eight million. Each year a torrent of immigrants pours in, over and beyond the recently acquired two Floridas. They nominate their representatives to the Congress in Washington in annual public meetings. The Congress convenes in the President's house until the Halls of Congress, destroyed by the English in the last war, can be rebuilt.[17] This choice falls for the most part on the more zealous and ardent patriots, who are also endowed with eminent qualities. The nominations are never made without heated debate and popular confrontations, because of the large number of emissaries hired by the Court of St. James who scheme continually to corrupt the republican spirit and reintroduce the monarchy. The candidates don't make a show of eloquent speech in dealing with public affairs, but rather display a wholesome logic and common sense intending to make the States prosper. Nor are any speakers ever denied attention, even though they should be anti-republicans, just as no expressions of blame or praise are pronounced on them. In a few words, they are models of wisdom and moderation, especially when they are treating of public affairs. President Madison completed his second four-year term in 1816, and his present successor is Monroe, who was indeed reconfirmed in his leadership for four more years at the beginning of 1821.[18] Tonchins was the Governor of New York at the time, and I was given his portrait.[19]

28   George Hayward,
Houses on William Street,
1800, lithograph.

Mauro's first lodgings
were about three blocks
south of the modest
residences shown here.

VIEW OF OLD BUILDINGS IN WILLIAM STREET.
looking from cor. of Liberty St. towards Maiden Lane N.Y. 1800.

FIRST LODGINGS IN
NEW YORK

Our Captain had referred me to a Mr. Durrant, who found lodgings for me with Mr. Perpignan[20] a shopkeeper at 26 William Street, across from the Post Office. As a special favor he granted me a room with a water closet, two beds, and some furniture for just thirteen dollars a month and, should I chose to dine in, for fourteen dollars a week for the two of us.[21] I preferred to take my meals with Mr. Chevalier in Chambers Street[22] since there I would have the opportunity to converse with a more varied group of people. His restaurant offered French cuisine,[23] and generally one paid a dollar and a half for a meal, excluding wine as is the custom everywhere, because this costs three dollars a bottle. In the whole of the United States they replace this blessed and inspiring beverage with whiskey, beer, rum, gin, and other strong liquors much diluted with water. Sometimes I was treated to refreshments consisting of one or two small glasses of Bordeaux, or Port or Madeira. In spite of this grave deficiency, nay, penury of wine I always provided myself and my companion with a couple of bottles a day.

SUCCESS OF MY LABORS

One day as I was walking along Broadway,[24] having a look at the luxurious shops, I read the name *Vecchio* on a sign. The Italian sound of it aroused in me the desire to meet the owner.

BROAD WAY FROM THE BOWLING GREEN.

He was from the Lake Como region, the youngest surviving brother of three. He owned a wealthy store where he sold mirrors, gilded furniture, and prints.[25] Then, without my intending it, he discovered that I was an artist and asked permission to pay me a visit. He arrived alone, and while he silently looked through my prints and drawings, now and again he would glance at me with an expression of surprise. I already mentioned to him that I had come to America strictly for pleasure. After he had done a little turn to the right, he bowed his head slightly and left. 'What manners!' said my companion. I laughed, and put my works away, intending to keep them buried. Half an hour later someone knocked at the door and, lo and behold, there was Mr.

William James Bennett,
*Broadway from the
Bowling Green*, c.1826,
aquatint.

The wealthy and
fashionable strolled this
residential section of
Broadway in the
afternoons.

Vecchio accompanied by five American gentlemen who were
curious to see my work. I consented to show it to them, and I
could occasionally hear, along with "bargain," the unmistakable
words: 'Beautiful, beautifully.' I dare tell you frankly that when
one of them picked up my engraving of Santa Cecilia and asked
me "How much cost?" (which means does it cost a lot? or should
it cost a lot?), I quoted him a price of 20 or 30 dollars.[26] This did-
n't seem to him, or to several others later on including some portrait painters, an excessive amount. I regretted that that I hadn't
brought more copies with me! I was offered 1,500 dollars for my
colored drawing *The Happy Dream*.[27] As the word spread around
from then on, I found myself besieged by a uninterrupted suc-
cession of notable people wanting either to acquire my work, or
to propose a commission, or who were simply curious. They
never left me a moment of peace. I cannot express the eagerness
with which Americans take an interest in those persons who, by
their intelligence or talent or ability are able to contribute to the
progress of the sciences and arts, and thus promote the greater
glory of the Nation. And in equal measure the felicitous inhabitants of this beautiful country foster among themselves an
extraordinary self-esteem. But in all truth I can assure you that,
even as they were competing to regale me with the products of
their invention, their gifts were always accompanied by ingenu-
ous protestations of recognition that the Italians, in particular,
had originated the models for these.

I decided then to leave my lodgings, situated in the centre
of town, and to seek another place much further away, where I
could devote myself to some work undisturbed. Having heard
that there was an apartment for rent in a stone house in Partition
Street, I betook myself there.[28] As I found the street door open,
I climbed up the staircase, which was covered by a wide band of
English carpet. Once at the top, I saw two entrance doors open.
I knocked, then I knocked again harder, and I called out in a
loud voice: Ohibo! No response. Ever eager to accomplish my
purpose, I walked right through the entire house stating repeatedly, "By your leave?" It was magnificently appointed with luxurious furnishings, and then I found myself in the entrance hall

once again. Disappointed, I returned to the person who had mentioned the house to me in the first place, and when I had recounted what had happened, he rebuked me sternly. "Well tell me, then," I rejoined, "Whenever does anyone leave his house unattended with the door open!" "I'll forgive you," he replied, "But you must learn that here one always knocks, and no one enters until someone inside gives him permission to do so. Should the owners have returned when you were in their home, you would have had a hard time trying to justify yourself with the Judge." Ever since then I have been very careful to follow their custom.

I had by then made myself comfortable in a small apartment of two rooms, a water closet and a kitchen rented to me by Mr. Gimbrede an engraver on the Bowery, No. 201, a good two miles from the center of this city which has no walls.[29] A wooden house with the same number of units as mine would cost four hundred and twenty dollars a year to rent. Gimbrede drew me here so that I could more comfortably contribute to some of the work he had begun, which included a portrait of General Jackson. The remoteness of my quarters did nothing to bring me a quieter life. Indeed, this pleasant boulevard being a popular promenade for New Yorkers, I was often honored by the visits of Mr. Trumbull, a member of the Academy;[30] Dickinson, a miniaturist; John Pintard, also a member of the Academy;[31] Murray, a member of the Government;[32] Doctor Mitchill, a professor of botany;[33] Stansbury;[34] Robertson, a painter;[35] Vanderlyn, just back from Paris;[36] Paff, a German merchant of fine art objects;[37] Sterling; Leney, the most accomplished engraver;[38] Dr. Main; de Soldati, an Italian; and a large number of other distinguished persons whom, for the sake of brevity, I shall omit.

The first of the persons mentioned above is the author of *The Sortie from Gibralter*, engraved by William Sharp in a classic print, and of other paintings engraved by others. The fourth work of a series had recently been finished. This represented the Declaration of Independence signed by the English and American plenipotentiaries, composed of twenty-six figures,

30   Asher B. Durand
(after John Trumbull),
*The Signing of the
Declaration of
Independence*, 1824,
engraving and etching.

An iconic moment in
American history was
widely known through
this engraving.

among whom were the immortal Washington, the venerable
Jefferson, the celebrated Franklin, Adams, and others, almost
all represented standing and dressed in the English fashion. He
proposed to me that I should execute the engraving after this
work, and offered me twenty thousand dollars for it. I gave
the matter serious reflection, and calculated that I would be engaged at the task for at least five years in order to execute so many
little portraits, so many boots, shoes, cravats, and twenty-six costumes in the French mode. I concluded that I would undoubtedly die of boredom before I could finish it. Furthermore, I
would need at least eleven thousand dollars to set up a house in
keeping with local custom, and the rest to maintain myself in the
luxury that etiquette required. So I refused this commission, as
honorable in subject as it was maladapted to an artist nourished
in the Italian school.

31   Detail of fig. 30.

There were too many little portraits and cravats for Mauro's taste.

MY OWN INVENTION

The honorable Mr. Collins, a Quaker as generous as he was gracious and a millionaire printer, visited me often, and was curious to see how a work of art came to be created.[39] He gave me a theme: "Moses Recovered from the Nile." I composed the image first on a slate, and then in watercolor on paper. Later he was kind enough to write to me in Florence, on 16 December 1816 from New York, proposing some work which, he said, would add lustre to a magnificent new bible. It is remarkable to see the insatiable effort and indefatigable zeal that the Quakers devote to their enterprises, for which they are willing to risk everything.

BEAUTIFUL HUMAN SPECIES

Throughout the United States the female sex displays an extraordinary beauty of the delicate kind. Climate and nutrition, far from corrupting the lovely English and Dutch species and their moral integrity, have indeed improved these races. The men themselves, who remind one of Antinuous and the Apollo Belvedere, inspire feelings of love, friendship, and respect, and the venerable old men radiate a sense of wisdom. As a rule, moderation and rigorous conduct rescue mankind from the tumult of its many passions which, by degrading the heart, succeed at last in corrupting physical appearance itself.

As I was setting up my studio in New York, I had a reading stand (which I still keep) made for me by a woodworker whose handsome features struck me. I never saw a more suitable head for the representation of the Saviour, or a King, or a Jove, and such a radiant complexion to boot. In short, the personification of the perfect man. He graciously charged me eight dollars for the stand, and I offered him up to sixteen dollars for a three or four hour sitting so that I could draw him, but he, overcome by excessive modesty, resolutely declined my offer and departed.

The custom of urinating in the streets is absent here, and their love of decency is carried so far that it is forbidden to even mention the word "breeches" in the presence of women. And don't think of mentioning what they cover! It is unusual, too, for a father to permit his daughter to remain in a family gathering when a stranger is visiting. The same applies to a husband in the case of his wife. It fell my lot to experience this one day when the eminent Dr. Bruce[40] had invited me to lunch with him at his home to give him the opportunity of obliging some of his learned friends who were eager participate in a discussion of the fine arts. I knew well that both his wife and his daughter were extraordinarily beautiful, and I counted on pleasing my fancy rather than my stomach. Wishful thinking! I had deluded myself. A slight indisposition served as a pretext for their absence.

If you wish to discover who had introduced such austere customs, it was the Quakers and not the English. Later on I shall say more of the former, but in the meantime I must tell you that a European who wants, or is obliged, to move in the cultivated sphere of society here must thoroughly reeducate himself, however well-bred he may be. The same sombre ceremony of masculine dining was repeated, however often I accepted an invitation. I ventured to ask why in the world, after showing such mutual trust in matters of commerce, they were so suspicious where women were concerned. They replied that we Italians were the "masters of women" in a sense quite contrary to their own. That is to say, that we take a wife to please others, whereas they do it only to please themselves. They noted further that to commit the crime of adultery, it's the initial encounter that counts.

PROSTITUTES

The first colonies felt very strongly the need to populate their vast territories. Marriage was the ready means at hand, not celibacy nor libertinage. Therefore in the whole of New York there were scarcely seven or eight loose women (excluding foreigners) at the time of my journey.[41] The affair is conducted behind closed doors, one deposits eight dollars then hastily satisfies one's sensual needs and leaves forthwith, neither person taking much notice of the other. An extraordinary number of sailors get married only to enjoy it for one fifth of their lives.

WHAT ONE EATS OF LITTLE ACCOUNT

Even the least affluent class of people refuses to perform household chores, so it is the blacks of both sexes who do them instead. One thing deserves mention here: the pleasures of the table are deemed of so little account that the Americans do not deign to practice the trade of cooking.[42] Even on board ships it is the blacks who do this. Meals consist of roast beef; beef steak and potatoes; or salted fish, peas, and beans, but never soup. Butter on bread and milk with tea or coffee are always in extreme moderation.[43] They are averse to delicacies, mixed fried foods, and the like, in short those foods that are dangerous to man's health. They are living proof that one should eat in order to live and not live to eat.

COMMERCE

And so what do their pleasures consist of, you may ask? Here they are: first of all in having broken the shameful fetters of servility, and by so doing maintaining their liberty, despite the efforts of their enemies. In watching their extraordinary maritime power grow stronger, and their lands prosper. In expanding their foreign commerce over the whole surface of the world, with flour, cotton, coffee, sugar, and wood for construction. In seeing themselves admired by the whole world, and increasing their population to such a degree that they are feared by every power on earth. In ornamenting their homes with luxurious furnishings of exquisite taste. And finally in the progress of the sciences, arts, and trades.

It seems fit here to call your attention to the lowest class of people. The innate longing for liberty on the one hand, and the greed to make a fortune on the other, attract the poor in particular. Furthermore, the news has spread from one pole to another that here a pair of shoes costs as much as eight dollars with the workmanship amounting to three dollars of this cost, fifteen dollars is the price of simple daily wear and one pays twelve for an ordinary chair, with the rest in proportion. And so now craftsmen from every corner of the globe are flocking here to make their fortunes.

ILLUSION OF MAKING A FORTUNE

One day as I was walking along a street, I heard someone call my name. I looked up, and saw someone peeking through a narrow opening in an attic. It was a certain Azam, a French shoemaker who had crossed the ocean with us, boasting of his expectations of an immense fortune in the United States. I gave in to his insistence, and climbed up to his miserable garret under the roof. His rich furnishings consisted of a cobbler's bench and some old shoe-lasts. He had already lived there two months. Astonished, I asked him what happened to his great fortune. "Ah! Mon cher Monsieur," replied he, "Elle est allée au cinq-cent-diables" ("Ah, my dear Sir, it's gone up in smoke"). He told me that the owner of the shoemaker's shop gave him barely enough to live on plus this miserable lodging.[44] He said that if he had brought with him a sum of money to set up home and shop, he would be in a position to do unto to others just what was being done to him, and so become rich. There are an infinite number of foreigners in that same condition. It is not given to every man to reach Corinth, so said the ancient Greeks.[45]

CHIMNEY SWEEPS

The blacks, shrewd and cunning, pay to rent the basements of the houses which, as is customary in Flanders, have access and light from the street. Here there reside a good few dozen workers. Thirteen dollars a week for a miserable straw pallet to sleep on, an ill-baked piece of bread, oysters and similar seafood sold from streetcarts,[46] and water distributed to the whole room once a day at the same hour, often constitute a cheap recourse for those who, to the detriment of their own persons, will suffer

32 (*facing page*)
Nicolino Calyo, *The Oyster Stand*, *c.*1840, watercolor.

Oysters, sold raw in shops or off carts, were the snack of choice for all classes of New Yorkers.

anything to make a living. On the subject of the blacks, the chimney sweepers are particularly curious. The master of some young colored boys goes about the streets brandishing a big stick, followed by one of these youngsters. The little one announces his trade not by cries, but rather with a trill and some musical notes, delivered with evident enthusiasm and in tunes that quite cheer the listener. I would often take pleasure in following along behind the ones who showed the most musical aptitude. These Africans are far more euphonious than the Americans.[47]

FREEING OF THE BLACKS

The United States coined a medal (which I still keep) with five allegorical figures, on the occasion of the freeing of the blacks. The inscription reads, "I have heard their afflictions, and abolished their servitude: 1807".[48] But then the blacks found themselves in a sorry plight because of their extreme ingratitude. They are obliged to serve for two or three years. They demand advances on their salaries. They desert, often stealing as they go,

33   Nicolino Calyo, *The Chimney Sweep at Rest*, c.1840, watercolor.

The ragged and exhausted chimney sweep was not always laughing and singing.

or else they arrogantly make trouble for their masters. Their women are even more petulant and treacherous than the men, and both sexes attest to the unreliable character of people from tropical climates.[49] These black women work as laundresses: each piece, large or small, brings them six Roman shillings, excluding blankets and sheets which cost three shillings a piece, or thirty-seven Roman shillings.

MONEY SYSTEM   It is appropriate now to give you an idea of their currency. One Spanish Dobloon, which weighs an ounce, is worth 15 dollars. The Golden Eagle, currency of the United States, is valued at 16 colonnati, half of one is 8. The Silver Eagle, which bears the insignia of liberty and as many stars as there are states in the Union, is worth 100 cents, or *soldi*, the half and the quarter in proportion. Schillings form an eighth part of the dollar, and are worth $12\frac{1}{2}$ cents.[50] Trading the gold coin at a bank for paper money, one makes a profit of 18 percent, for the silver one, 14 percent, but if you wish to trade paper money for coins, you lose more than 18 percent and 14 percent respectively, the difference in proportion to the exchange rate on the current market. The paper money of Philadelphia is worth less than that of New York.

CLIMATE   Today, 15 June 1822, I have the pleasure of obliging your questions by writing you this loose-knit letter concerning climate. Here in Milan we are already beaten down and oppressed by the heat. I observe the Réaumur thermometer in my studio, and it points, after noon, to almost 21 degrees and outside in the shade to 26½. In New York, during the same month in 1816, in one bedroom that had cooled down during the night, the daytime temperature rose to 29, and outside to 32. One felt this suffocating heat viscerally, as you can imagine. Plenty of pineapples, the famous coconut milk, and the coolest water barely sufficed to mitigate such a heat. Then came an unexpected change and the thermometer plunged to 17 degrees above zero, then it suddenly went up again. Such a pernicious alternation of climate was frequent, and the inhabitants of the city were prone to serious chest colds and bronchitis. The shopkeepers, outside their homes, kept overcoats at hand to protect themselves as the occasion demanded. The physical reason for this inconstancy of temperature is that the maritime coast is densely inhabited and covered with cities, but lacks a chain of mountains that would shelter it from the winds so that when the Mexican, or the equator, winds blow you burn up, and when these grow silent, then the Canadian or Greenland winds freeze you. The winters are so rigorous, so they told me, that in those rooms that are heated by stoves during the day even five blankets on the bed at night hardly serve one's needs, and that is why vineyards and olive groves don't thrive here. Only Carolina, Georgia, and Florida along with some other regions in the west can sustain them. Nevertheless, the air is generally salubrious and the sky is beautiful. The countryside offers a picturesque and gracious aspect, thanks to the contrast between the woods and still virgin forests, and the cultivated lands. The number of farmers was then very small in proportion to the vast terrain and the number of consumers, but the fertility of the land provided well for the needs of the people.

SOLEMN CELEBRATION OF
THE REPUBLIC

When the memorable date of the Fourth of July came, I witnessed with sincere pleasure their solemn yet tumultuous festival of independence. For this anniversary the citizen members of the National Guard had intensified their training in military exercises. At nine o'clock in the morning a well-ordered procession set forth and paraded through the main quarters of the city. The hearts of these free people were inflamed by a portrait of Washington, their Brutus.[51] It was painted on a canvas carried aloft like a banner, along with those of Columbus, Vespucci, Franklin, Jefferson, and numerous other of their philosopher-heroes who had contributed to their liberty and their expansion.[52] Among these images were various symbols pulled on carts that alluded to freedom, equality, justice, and courage. Some of these were single representations, others loomed from under small temples which contained faded wooden busts and sculptures.[53] Interspersed with all these objects stood guards on picket duty. I posted myself in front of City Hall under some beautiful trees so that I could see the main part of the Guard and the artillery parade by, promising myself that at

34   Baron Axel
Leonhard
Klinckowström,
*Broadway Street and the
City Hall*, 1819, aquatint.

Trees in the City Hall
Park afforded shade for
the pedestrians, but
roaming pigs were ever
in evidence.

35 John Hill (after William Guy Wall), *New York City Hall*, 1826, aquatint.

The New York City Hall can be seen today much as it was recorded by this observer.

the same time I would also see public officials in full regalia.[54] The great balustrade porch, the balconies, and the steps were all teeming with people, but there were no magistrates in formal dress. So I questioned Mr. Murray, whom I chanced to find close by, and he answered that on this day homage was paid only to the site where law and justice are asked and executed, but not to their enforcers, who are always considered the equals of others.[55] Their musical bands were rather good. As I left the enclosed area to watch the august ceremony from the Port, what a surprise awaited me! Would you believe it? The procession was brought to an close that year by a gorgeous barge that rested on several carts pulled by a large number of horses. It was handsomely painted and built of solid wood, in the same proportion to the real thing as a four-year-old child is to a grown man. A good number of children, dressed up as sailors and well-rehearsed, pretended to execute various marine manoeuvres around the suspended sails and poles. I swear to you that I couldn't contain my tears of pleasure for the intense emotions that I felt.[56]

THE SERVANTS ARE SERVED
    You should take note, furthermore, that on this day the servants do not serve their masters, but rather the other way around.[57] Throughout the whole affair, orderliness prevailed and there was no threat to authority, although on such an occasion

the populace, one might say, revels in a frenzy. All along the broad avenues of Battery Park,[58] which borders the Hudson River, towards the triangular-shaped City Hall and along other public roads as far as Long Island, one found stalls with marquees where they sold food and drinks. The trades' masters had been given the job of insuring the orderliness of the parade, and they wore a little red ribbon in their buttonholes as a distinctive mark, indicating that they had to be obeyed by everyone else. It is a universal custom to celebrate this day all across the United States, but in no city with such enthusiasm as in New York. The means of government surveillance on this day is the same as usual, meaning that the policemen, wearing no exterior distinction, confront the troublemaker. They brandish a small black stick with an ivory handle as is customary in England and threaten him in the name of the law to consider himself under arrest.[59] If he refuses, he is forced to do so by the people. Layabouts and loafers are detested in these parts, and hypocrisy would be hard put to insinuate itself here. Everyone hates it at least as much as I do.

MASKS ARE FORBIDDEN   Apart from this singular event, the populace never gathers for revelry. The Government, in its wisdom, prohibits it. Indeed in 1816 an association of French speculators betook themselves to the Governor to propose to him a project. This was a plan to introduce balls and fancy-dress parties during the Carnival. They marshalled all the seductive power of their eloquence. The Governor allowed them to exhaust their fine words, then he set himself to asking them coldly what crimes they were planning to commit since they intended to make themselves unrecognizable by wearing masks on their faces. The petitioners, perplexed, were pondering their response when the Governor rose to his feet, "Leave here at once, and shame on you for suggesting the surest way to corrupt the morals of the United States," he thundered.[60]

In New York there is only one public garden, which at night is illuminated like the European Vauxhall. The rooms I saw there were decorated simply with plain geographical and marine maps, and were places where one could drink various kinds of refreshments. This too is a business run by a

Frenchman, and overseen very closely by the Government, meaning the Police.[61]

One of their notable customs is the way merchants display their goods outside their shops. For instance, the rarest objects from the East Indies and other precious items might lie on a couple of tables unguarded. They simply trust everyone to be honest. "And although it is rarer than comets to witness a burglary," it so happened one day that an unemployed Irishman put his hands on a roll of fabric as if intending to steal it. He was seized by the people (as is customary) and taken to Court. The Court found him guilty, as they generally found guilty any Irishman who was out of work and without visible means of support. They sent him to till the land in the furthermost ends of the States. The capital crimes of robbery, assault, and homicide are resolved not after a lapse of several years, but within a few days with the gallows.[62] Their judgments are based on principles that are simpler even than those of the English. Each state, however, adjusts its municipal laws to accord with the qualifications of their local police force, but in no instance do they deviate from the principle of severity. In this country, he who confesses his crime is not regarded as a madman, nor is it required that witnesses had been present. In August 1816, a sailor who had killed his adversary with pistol shot in the heat of a fight was hanged,[63] but you should take note that in the whole of the United States it had been four years since the last capital crime had taken place. The riff-raff settles its quarrels as in England, with a fist-fight. The populace takes it upon itself to act as spectator, second, and judge all at once.

A large stone building, recently constructed two miles away from the town along an arm of the sea that separates the peninsula from Long Island, is used as a hospice for the poor and as a place of detention or punishment at the same time.[64] The former are treated with the utmost humanity, but the prisoners are forced to labour ceaselessly in order to supplement the expense of daily food and the maintenance of the place. Many old people and helpless widows are reduced to living there of their

36 Anonymous, *Alms House Hospital, Bellevue as City Penitentiary*, *c.*1820, lithograph.

This institution housed together, for better or worse, the destitute, the aged, and the criminal.

own accord in order to have enough to eat, as begging is forbidden everywhere.

CLEMENCY FOR DEBTORS

In order to punish debtors, three boundaries are drawn around the main commercial center, which takes as its focal point the City Hall. Each of the three is coordinated with a fixed debt level. The debtor who owes the least is not allowed to enter the central delimitation, and is punished if he does. Others who owe more are excluded from the second and third areas, according to the amount of their debts.[65] This is the equivalent of our saying that a major debtor is exiled outside the walls of St. Lazarus and those of the old Roman Road.[66] If he is caught in the act of trespassing by an Inspector, he is arrested at once. Even then he is not deprived of the means to redeem himself. A debtor who defaults is condemned to imprisonment in the Tower, or a gaol, whence he can speak to those outside from its balcony and attempt to find a way to settle his debts.

CAUSE OF THE BANKRUPTCIES

Bankruptcy is quite frequent, especially in New York, and the bankrupts find no less leniency than the debtors. This kind of serious financial and social failure can be traced to the fervid passion to get rich that predominates and lures people to risk their all.[67] With shiploads of immense value transported from the

STAGECOACH (RAPID
TRANSPORT)

West to the East Indies and from one pole to the other over
the treacherous oceans, many fortunes are lost. Another cause is
the frequency of fires in their wooden houses. They have counted
up to three hundred and fifty or four hundred fires in New York
each year. Every night we were awakened by the cries, "Fire, fire,
gentlemen!", which incites the ever-helpful Americans to rush to
the aid of their compatriots, their hearts pounding in their
chests.[68] This serious disgrace should disappear within a few
years, thanks to a modern law which dictates that the houses shall
be built of stone.[69]

Once I had got my companion accustomed to buying the daily
groceries at the market and to cooking at home, I decided to
venture alone into the interior of the country, leaving her with all
the necessary provisions. I took advantage of the offer of some
friends from Philadelphia to visit this richest and most beautiful
city in the United States, about one hundred and twenty
miles south of New York. To this end, I had my name registered
at a Post Office, or Stagecoach company. The stagecoaches
are long and low vehicles on four wheels, with four benches

38 (*above*) Anne-Marguérite-Henriette Rouillé de Marigny, Baroness Hyde de Neuville, *Corner of Greenwich and Dey Streets*, 1810, watercolor.

Wooden houses such as these were fuel for the raging city fires. The World Trade Center towers later stood here.

37 (*facing page*) Anne-Marguérite-Henriette Rouillé de Marigny, Baroness Hyde de Neuville, *Bridewell, and Charity School, Broadway*, 1808, watercolor.

A modest pedestrian stretch of Broadway with the Bridewell Prison looming behind.

39 (*right*) Nicolino Calyo, *The Head Foreman*, c.1840, watercolor.

The fire-chief exhorts his team and local citizens to action.

The Head Foreman

across, and with eight poles or staffs supporting a sheet of leather as a roof and sliding leather curtains on the sides. They hold sixteen people with their small pieces of luggage and are pulled by four beautiful horses, driven by an highly capable coachman.

EASE OF TRAVEL   Nothing is so economically priced as travelling in this country. Going from New York to Philadelphia costs a mere eight dollars, and the expense of getting to intermediate places or those beyond is calculated proportionately.[70]

CITY OF NEWARK   I first reserved a place on the stagecoach for the burgeoning city of Newark, which essentially consisted of two long rows of wooden houses, elegantly built and painted the color of ashes. The next morning at dawn I was taken to the opposite shore of the Hudson river on a steamboat, where our coach awaited us.[71] My only travelling companions as far as Newark were a lady and her little girl. During the trip, as we went deeper into the virgin forests once inhabited by the primitive Illinois and Iroquois, I began to satisfy my curiosity about the countryside.

PLANTS AND TREES   I observed a great variety of shrubs, flowers, and herbaceous plants, still partly unknown to us. There were trees with lofty trunks, which we would consider exotic, such as the sycamores, the beautiful tiger maples of Pennsylvania and Canada, the Virginia poplars, and the witch hazels, whose resin has veterinary properties. There were plane trees and huge passion flowers, locust trees and many others which, in their maturity, seem to touch the clouds. They grow higher in America than in our country, which is their adopted one. The massive *Buxus semper vivans*, whose hardness sets it as a connecting link in the great chain of woods and metals, and as suitable as they for engraving, is found in abundance.

QUADRUPEDS AND BIRDS   In the vicinity of Brunswick, another little town, I saw a local variety of cow without horns and of a singular shape. I noticed also, near some farmers, some sheep whose tail alone can weigh up to fifty pounds. I also saw stags, deer, squirrels, and large reptiles. Among the birds I admired some varieties of woodpeckers of extraordinary beauty, whose plumage is comparable to that of the parrot family.[72]

40 Detail of
fig. 37.

No fashionable
promeneurs here,
only a boy carrying
a mug of beer, an
errant pig, and
washing hung out
to dry.

AGRICULTURE   Farmers here dress with such elegance and neatness that they
are barely distinguishable from the richer landowners. Although
they prove themselves far inferior to us in agriculture, that
noblest of pursuits, nevertheless they have some machinery and
rural equipment with which we are unfamiliar and which is
extremely useful. They fell the ancient forests, and if the ground
is found to be sufficiently flat they flood it with water so that the
tree-stumps rot, forming an organic fertilizer which, over a period of years, is supplemented by ashes. Until 1816 they never used
animal manure. One day, in conversation with a French farmer,
he pointed to a piece of land, little more than a short turn from
the town, that he had bought thirty years before for only 13 dollars, but which would sell today for 250. Firewood also becomes
more expensive from day-to-day, because it is harvested but
never replanted thus diminishing the supply, a practice
which raises the price appreciably. In the whole State of New

York, the custom of grafting has not yet been introduced. In Pennsylvania, however, one can eat some excellent fruit grown this way. The southern states and the Islands, as I noted, furnish a large amount of delightful fruit. One of their customs, which I dare say rouses admiration, has to do with their fences. They split trees into four parts or even more, and once they have removed the bark, they trim them down to a uniform length of four yards. Then they join them together in serpentine fashion. Each proprietor strives to make his fence-weaving pattern different from the others in order to distinguish his boundaries and demonstrate his skill. At the same time the fences serve as a meandering and pleasant ornament to the smiling countryside. They place some tightly woven frames made of thin wooden sticks around the necks of their small animals so that they can't get through the fences, especially the pigs which they allow to wander through the streets.[73] They use horses to plough the fields and for other farm work, so their cattle are free to produce the very best milk products and beef.

BRIDGE AT TRENTON

Then having satisfied my curiosity on these matters, after a few days I took the stagecoach again. By giving a one dollar tip I arranged to stop over at Trenton so that I could observe at leisure the famous wooden bridge over the river there. This bridge is over twenty perches long.[74] There are no piers of any kind to support it, nor does it rest on arches. The weight of this monumental construction is borne by thick iron chains, skilfully stretched and fixed at both ends, thus forming a long and spacious gallery covered by an eaved roof to shelter it from the intemperate heavens. The framework of the walls is formed by a number of wooden arches which support the roof and cross in such a manner that the weight is distributed toward the extremities and plays itself out against the two stone bridgeheads. Some small windows are cut through the walls to allow some light into the interior. The road through the center is wide enough to permit two vehicles to pass. The other two lateral ones are to accommodate pedestrians. The inevitable concave spaces left between the thick chains are skilfully boxed in by large wooden slabs, which on the exterior display an architrave. The two entrances, or rather gateways, are of cut stone in good architectural style. No other structure of a similar nature and comparable from many points of view, is more solid and costs less to maintain than this one. Nevertheless two guards oversee the entrances to remind the cart drivers to make haste. As I mentioned before, in each village and settlement that the stagecoach passes on its way, a change of passengers takes place. Half way between New York and Philadelphia the stagecoach stopped over for the night, and so did I, in a place that thanks to its elegant service and its decor resembles a delightful country inn rather than a tavern. They charge 1¾ dollars for dinner and for the bed, as I remarked in more detail earlier.

THE YOUNG CREOLE   The following morning at daybreak, I was pleasantly surprised to discover that my only travelling companion in the stagecoach was a young Creole woman, that is to say the daughter of a native American man and an English woman. That mixture of these two physiognomical types so widely different, I swear to you, gave her features an indescribable mixture of the picturesque and singular, so much so as to silence my fifty years of age. Oh, what a distracting conversation we enjoyed for a good hour of the journey! Then other people came on board, and unfortunately the beautiful native disappeared from my sight.

With the stagecoach crowded with people, we were approaching at full gallop the third city, which bears the beautiful name of brotherly love, when I saw some children who were being taught to swim in a ditch of stagnant water (as swimming is the first skill that these people learn). Turning to my neighbor, a Milady of a certain age and a mother herself, I said, "Look at those boys." No sooner had she glanced towards them than, with an abrupt movement, she turned her back on them disdaining, from an excess of modesty, to look upon naked bodies.[75] "Alas!" I said to myself, "Painting will never find a good home here!", as indeed I shall prove to you shortly.

CITY OF PHILADELPHIA   Now I shan't say to you, my dear friend, that I have three thousand years under me, as a modern traveller who had passed the night on top of an Egyptian pyramid has written,[76] but I can nonetheless say that I am proud of having lived in the most beau-

41   William Birch, *View in Third Street from Spruce Street, Philadelphia*, 1799, etching.

Philadelphia at this time surpassed New York in sophistication and refinement.

tiful and richest city of the West Indies, the youngest city in the world, and at the same time the most venerable for its virtues and customs.[77] It appeared, if I may say so, like some wooden larva scarcely a hundred years ago, and in a flash, within the space of thirty years, has undergone its metamorphosis, transforming itself into the most perfect example of a city. The famous Dutch philosopher W. Penn,[78] the leader of the Colony, established the city's borders not far from the Delaware River, fixed its central point, and traced the two main roads, which intersect from North to South, and from East to West. Nor do their subsidiary roads deviate from this rectilinear grid, and nowadays bear names relating to it such as Second or Fourth Street North, Third Street or Eleventh Street East, with the houses being numbered. These are of a simple and uniform style on the outside, and are three storeys high at most. They are all of a reddish tint, and the mortar between the bricks is highlighted with white which lends a graceful note of color to the local ambience.[79] The many temples and banks are not constructed in this fashion. They all vaunt their wealth and magnificent architecture, and no expense is spared, be it millions of dollars.[80] These edifices are for the most part built of white marble or other carved stone. Imagine for a moment the astonishing contrast produced by so many monuments of various architectural styles, among the monotonous and modest regularity of the surrounding houses, which seem to have been built only to serve as a scenographic backdrop for the monuments. And this is not all: each house is separated from its neighbour by an alleyway, closed at the front by a gate parallel with the façade of the house, and closed only by a simple latch. This alley is used bring household goods and firewood into the backyard. Generally the houses are provided with a small patch of land cultivated as a vegetable and flower garden and at the end of which is situated the

42   William Birch, *The Bank of the United States, Philadelphia (later Girard's Bank)*, 1798, etching.

The impressive marble facade of this bank stood in contrast to the plain clapboard building next door.

GIRARD'S BANK, late the

BANK of the UNITED STATES, in Third Street   PHILADELPHIA.

43   William Birch, *High Street from Ninth Street, Philadelphia*, 1799, etching.

The wide streets and planned city differed sharply from the colorful chaos of New York.

outhouse. And because around here it is forbidden to urinate, etc., in the streets, anybody is allowed access to other people's toilets by way of the above-mentioned garden gates to satisfy their pressing needs.[81] This friendly arrangement is compensated in good measure by the cleanliness of the town itself. What a disgrace it is, the soiling of walls and public streets that is unfortunately practiced in our country. Not even the sacred temples are spared such ignominy! And Oh! How often did I hear Americans and other non-Catholic travellers tell me that they were deceived by their appearance into thinking that these monuments were magnificent toilets!

Returning to the subject of the beautiful districts of Philadelphia, I shall tell you that on the outside corners of the houses, just at the entrance of the dividing alleyway, they plant a tall tree. It may be a glorious plane tree, or a *Heterophyllous Aylantus*, a Babylonian willow, or a slender cypress, a trembling poplar, or similar trees that grow higher than the roof, providing shade and a pleasant ornament during the summer season. Alongside each road are

44   William Birch, *The High Street Country Market*, 1799, etching.

Outdoor markets with produce from the rich Pennsylvania farmland thrive in Philadelphia today.

two broad paved sidewalks, raised two hand-spans above the ground. Ordinarily on either side of the houses' doors there are square gardens surrounded by low and simple lattice fences made of wood, and their security is assured by the honesty of the citizens. Everyone competes to show off to the passers-by his most beautiful flowers, fragrant herbs, and climbing plants that adorn the windows of his first floor. Imagine what a seductive and delightful perspective greets the eye of the foreigner when he finds himself face to face with one of these long, straight streets. It often seemed to me more like a pleasant dream than reality, and I cannot deny having felt an involuntary twinge of envy, born of love for my native country.[82]

PHILADELPHIA MARKET

A sumptuous building, half a mile long and located in the center of town, halfway up the broadest street, Market Street, accommodates the vendors of food-products. It features a large covered walkway, which is raised five or six steps above ground level.[83] The merchants are lined up along the two sides, leaving the center free for the buyers. The entire length of the street is divided into a number of sections, each of which contains all the various kinds of vendors, and a sampling of all the products for sale. In this way, the inhabitants of the east end of town don't have to go all the way to the west end of the market, and the same for those who live in center-town. Philadelphia has a fairly good theater, but I didn't see any performances as summer is the holiday season.[84] It also has an academy of science and a library. Despite the preponderance of Quakers, foreigners are here less subject to the austere social proprieties than elsewhere. Furthermore, the food is better, the fruit tastier, and in general living costs are lower. Being further south, its climate is milder than in New York.

My good friend Moses Thomas, publisher of the *Analectic Magazine* in Chestnut Street N. 52 and a millionaire Quaker, had, while in New York, frequently encouraged me to settle here. He offered me the good services of his home.[85] I was unwilling to deviate from my sacred principle of independence, however, and had chosen to lodge with a certain Madame Fillette. I nevertheless accepted the services of one of his young booksellers as a guide. I went immediately to the City Hall which was not made of white marble like the one in New York and is very simple in its three main structures. The two lateral wings are higher than the central one and the whole thing is red brick.[86] Beyond the court room, another room above it on the second floor has been designated to house the collection of natural history.[87] These spaces thus contain everything that is considered the rarest and most instructive from the animal, vegetable, and mineral kingdoms. Furthermore, the collections are rich in all that concerns the works of the native people of America, and well-stocked in equipment and instruments for the use of the sciences such as physics, optics, navigation, and so forth. The French Government, under the Consulate of Napoleon, enriched this establishment with many a useful and precious object. Alongside these are several oil portraits which I recognised at first sight.[88] Here I saw the entire skeleton of an enormous mastodon, whose species no longer exists, in excellent condition and much larger in size than the biggest Asian elephant.[89] A painting documented the phenomenon of a black man who

45   William Birch, *The Back of the Statehouse with Indians*, 1799, etching.

Philadelphia brick architecture, its park peopled by a variety of casual passers-by.

had suffered a disease that turned his skin perfectly white. In a smaller room I was able to observe also several fine anatomical paintings.[90] The cabinet is splendidly equipped with examples of ornithology, cetaceans, and insects typical of the New World, but it remains inferior to European cabinets in many respects, especially as concerns the mineral kingdom and crystals. To gain access one buys an entrance ticket for the sum of three quarters of a dollar.

ACADEMY OF FINE ARTS

PHILADELPHIA

The following day Mr. Thackara, Director of the Academy of Fine Arts, honored me with his generosity by giving me free access to this beautiful place.[91] A large iron gate that gives onto the street marks the entrance to a spacious garden, allowing one to enjoy the view of the façade and the peristyle of the building. The first gallery is almost as large as the ground floor. Well lit, it contains the casts of ancient sculptures given by Bonaparte, some prints and models, and a few studies made and left behind by the students. I had the pleasure of seeing, framed and on the wall, my engraving after Guido Reni's *Madonna*, and my *Saint Cecilia*, the latter being more appreciated here than the former

because it shows less nudity.[92] An ample staircase leads up to the
second gallery, which is higher. It is in the shape of a rotunda,
illuminated like the Pantheon, and the whole complex breathes
an air of magnificence. It contains a good number of oil paintings, both old and new. West, who was born in America, has
given them one of his large paintings, but not his masterpiece.[93]
Bonaparte donated a beautiful Poussin, Reynolds gave one of his
works. Mr. Leslie, an excellent portraitist,[94] gave a portrait, and
other zealous contributors provided several pieces from the
Venetian school (which so far is the only one that is moderately
well-known here), with which they have adorned this picture
gallery. There are a few half-length portraits of women, none
showing an arm or the juncture of the neck, and least of all an
uncovered breast, excluding French women and other foreigners.
A certain Newton from Boston, a portraitist, is supreme in this
genre of painting.[95]

One Alston [*sic*], a young student, has donated one of his
huge paintings which represents a dead man resuscitated.[96] The
more the good Thackara strove, though in vain, to reveal its sublime beauties to me, the easier it was for me to prove their utter

absence, if veracity and common sense should be qualities inseparable from good painting. For the love of the truth, I added that good historical painters would never emerge in their country unless first they overcame the puerile prejudice against studying the nude body. Then, albeit in jest, I thought to add that it would be a greater miracle to correct the distorted limbs of the resuscitated man than to bring him back to life. The good Quaker Director couldn't resist the evidence of my reasoning, but being an impassioned lover of decency more than of art, he replied, "Well, perhaps some day even we will become good painters." "How many students do you have?", I then asked him, and he replied, "One and a half," (as they often speak figuratively), meaning that the first one studied every day, whereas the other studied only every other day. "What amazing naivety," I said to myself, "But what a pity that, in a country where all the beauty of the human species is preeminently displayed, no artist should avail himself of it!"

PRINTMAKERS   You should know that here everything is driven by the principle of speculation, so when the most renowned printmakers of the Philadelphia establishment, Fairman, Murray, Draper, etc.,[97] learned of my arrival, they did me the honor of proposing an association with them as draughtsman and printmaker. But since the whole business is reduced to vignettes, allegories, invoices, and the smallest copper plates to use in their Bible, or some little portrait, thanking them from the bottom of my heart I disengaged myself.

RESTAURANTS   I very much enjoyed the dinner hour at Mme Fillette's, whose husband did the honors and made the rounds of the tables in the French manner.[98] This admirable family emigrated from Santo Domingo during the revolution instigated by Toussaint l'Ouverture. Thanks to their jovial manners and good prices, as well as their welcoming hospitality, they attract foreign visitors who are gravitating toward Philadelphia less than elsewhere.

QUAKERS   If I am not mistaken, the reason is as follows. In the first place, since the city's population is two thirds Quaker, its moral tone is too permeated by a mood of sobriety to please the generality of foreigners. The Quakers' clothes do not change throughout the

47   Nicolino Calyo, *A Quakeress*, c.1840, watercolor.

The simplicity and severity of the Quakers that Mauro both admired and deplored is reflected in their dress.

year in cut or color. The men's consist of a tight-fitting coat the color of ashes, open in the front; a shirt; trousers; white stockings; shoes; a collar; and a round, wide-brimmed hat that in the summer is made of straw. The monsters of fashion and fanaticism have never dwelt among them, and they have never been gripped by the obsession with fashion and its blind enthusiasms. Averse to amusement and methodical in their business, they manifest everywhere a rigorous judgmentalism which in the end becomes utterly monotonous.[99] In the second place, as financial fortunes are better established here than elsewhere, with the core of the wealth concentrated in the Quakers' hands, commerce is less lucrative for ensconced speculators, though it is also less likely to end in bankruptcy. Tranquillity and security have taken root here, and I like to call it the city of the rich philosopher. As a natural consequence there are few lovers of luxury, and thus the number of jewellers is quite limited. I saw only one well-stocked shop of this precious merchandise. It is the venture of a certain Mr. Chaudron, a Frenchman.[100] I followed my inclination to walk inside, and asked the price of a two carat diamond. He replied that it cost 34 dollars, his fixed price. "So", I said to myself, "That's almost double what it would cost in Bologna". And while, to the contrary, they hold in less esteem the eastern and western colored stones, I made a good profit by exchanging my diamonds for opals, rubies, sapphires, emeralds, and other precious stones that are highly prized among us, especially when they are faultless.[101]

SCHUYLKILL SUBURB   One day, as I sat at my usual table, a good old immigrant was trying to tempt me to think no longer of my homeland but to join some of his friends who were determined to create and populate new cities in the vast and uncultivated American lands. "What ever would I do, my dear friend," I replied, "With my engraving tools and my brushes?" "Vous nous aiderez á tracer des plans topographiques et á propager l'espèce" ("You will help us draw topographical maps and propagate the species"). "Vous me faites beaucoup d'honneur" ("You do me much honor"), I rejoined. Indeed, not long after this I learned that the Government of the United States had sold one hundred and fifty thousand acres of land in the Mississippi territories, along with the native tribes that lived there, to his society at two dollars per acre (a measurement roughly equivalent to forty-one tornature, or Emilian hectares). The sum was to be paid within fourteen years, on condition however that they introduce the cultivation of vineyards and olive trees.[102]

I then determined to explore the more beautiful outlying areas, so I went over towards the suburb of Schuylkill, at the top end of which one finds the first hydraulic machine, or pump, that is steam powered.[103] It draws water from the limpid river that gives its name to the suburb, and distributes it directly to the city-dwellers by means of subterranean pipes of welded iron. This construction is undoubtedly one of the most beautiful, adorned on the outside by a magnificent rotunda with graceful grotesques and panoramic terrace. The water descends then into a great reservoir of fresh water.[104] It was the mating season for the various amphibians including the frogs, who intensified the atmosphere of the site by their croaking among the marsh

48   R. Campbell (after Thomas Birch), *View of the Dam and Water Works at Fair Mount, Philadelphia*, 1824, engraving.

A panoramic view of Philadelphia's impressive system of water collection and delivery.

49   Anonymous, *The Promenade at the Fairmount Waterworks*, c.1836, lithograph.

The vistas and paths at the Fairmount Park remained a favorite spot for visitors throughout the nineteenth century.

plants. At that time, in that part of the garden, it had been possible to build only a shabby wooden cabin, and there were also the ruins of another that had burned down. A few steps away from the road there was a wonderful tower, known as the tower of lead because it was where they made the lead shots for hunters.[105] Not far from here one came across another wooden bridge[106] over the Schuylkill similar to the one I already described over the Trenton, and then another outdoor pump whose water is also channelled down to the city.

Finally, about four miles further on, I arrived at the best-known botanical garden in the United States, courtesy of Mr. Morris.[107] The location of this vast establishment is at the same time pleasant and geographically appropriate by virtue of the

50   Baron Axel Leonhard Klinckowström, *Upper Ferry Bridge, Schuylkill River,* c.1819, aquatint.

The famous "Colossus" bridge downstream from the Fairmount dam.

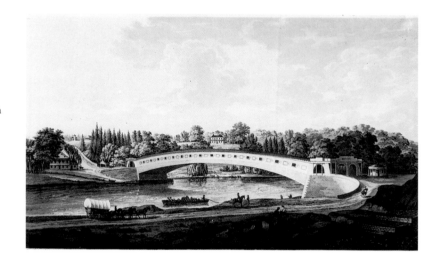

51   A. Lawson (after John James Barralet), *North View of the Schuylkill Bridge* etching.

An industrial, rather than scenic, aspect of the river with the bridge in the distance.

irregularity of the terrain and the abundant means of irrigation.
One is not required to pay an entrance fee. I praised heaven and
Mr. Morris for this, and other respectable folk who had found
their ways there, as happened daily, smiled with me. The two
well-informed gardeners, who ordinarily explained the beautiful
and extensive vegetable kingdom to ignorant and dull people,
were taken aback when they realized that I knew the plants by
their scientific names according to the Linnaean system.
Henceforth they showed a particular regard towards me, while
the others, probably millionaires, trailed along behind me, a
mere European. Among the plants that had been discovered
only recently, and which are still unknown to us, the one that
pleased me most was an agave of a deep purple colour.[108] It hadn't
yet produced shoots, so I was unable to procure for my country something of such rarity. I was, however, presented with a
variety of precious seeds and, content to have spent a most deli-
cious day in the New World, I made my way back to the city.

NATIVE PEOPLE   I then lost no time in satisfying my curiosity on a matter of
the greatest interest to me, which was to see at first hand the
primitive tribes of the West Indies, that species of mankind that
so captivates the mind of the philosopher, in order to determine
for myself their true nature. Oh, how many ideas flooded into
my poor head! But this subject is one worthy of you, my friend,
who possesses in abundance the resources and the eloquence to
describe the varieties of mankind. However that may be, the fact
remains that from time to time the native Illinois gather here in
groups of six, eight, or ten, loaded down with their furs or leather
to exchange for aquavit, liquors, nails, and various iron tools. On
these occasions the more civilized natives, or their Creole children, act as interpreters for the negotiations. Since the natives
don't care for luxury, their way of dressing consists of wrapping
an animal skin around their waist, with another larger one serving as a cloak. This is fastened by straps and covers their shoulders, back, chest, and half their legs. They wear a kind of stock-
ing on their feet and some, particularly the Chief, have a tuft of
multicolored feathers on their heads. They all have the well-
known hieroglyphic characters painted on their skins, and they

52 (*above left*) Detail of fig. 45.

53 (*above right*) Anne-Marguérite-Henriette Rouillé de Marigny, Baroness Hyde de Neuville, *Tonavente, Peter of Bufalo, an Iroquois of the Niagara Region, c.*1810, watercolor.

A sympathetic rendering of a native of one of the Iriquois tribes, evidently drawn from life.

shave, or rather pull out their entire beards as well as their hair, leaving only a bit down the middle of their scalps. Their physiognomy has a well defined character, different from other races which are, as you know, the Caucasian (European), East Indian, Chinese, and African. I drew the profiles of two of them as they negotiated their merchandise. The most characteristic features of their faces are their rather prominent cheekbones, and the downturned corners of their mouths. Their eyes are dark and lively, and their skin a dark gold. The women are extremely obedient to their husbands. They tie their nursing babies to a board hung by a strap that passes across their foreheads, and thus they carry the babes, hanging on their backs, on the longest journeys and through the most fatiguing labors while the men occupy themselves hunting with bow and arrow, and with war, their sole art and science. The women build the huts and the pirogues, or canoes, which are light rowboats formed from a tree trunk and covered with skins. These races, like their neighbours the Iroquois, show a disposition as peaceful towards strangers as it is ruthless against their enemies in times of war.[109] There is no kind of torture that they will not inflict on their prisoners. These, for their part, bear the long agonies inflicted on them with an amazing strength of character, priding themselves on being unmatched in their heroic courage. They will sooner die than utter a cry.

I shall pass now into the shadowy realm of mystery and touch on religion. It is an appropriate subject to discuss in this town, as it is here, in fact, that one finds the greatest number of churches of various sects. Since the spirit of this immense family is founded on the principle of tolerance for everything that is, to their way of thinking, purely a matter of opinion, it follows that freedom of thought is regarded by them as a sacred yet intangible heritage bequeathed to us by Nature from the moment of our birth, a precious gift of which nobody has the right to deprive us. So here they have a pact of reciprocal respect. Whatever their preferred formal ceremonies and religious customs may be, they are tolerated provided, however, that these are practiced exclusively within the respective temples of each sect. Because of this an imperturbable social harmony reigns among them, free of resentment and hatred. Here I had the opportunity of observing as many as twenty varieties of religion and about forty churches. There were Jews and many varieties of Christians: Episcopalians, Roman Catholics, Reformed, Quakers, Reformed Lutherans, Calvinists, Methodists, Associated, Swedish Lutherans, Confederates, Universalists, Independents, Unitarians, Indifferents, Moravians, Free Quakers, and German Reformed.[110] Note, however, that he who professes no religion at all would not enjoy such a good reputation among the Americans. The Free-Masons also have their own temple, built in the Gothic style, which is both spacious and beautiful. They don't admit foreigners during their services.

The Quakers, I should tell you, were the ones that most excited my curiosity. Listen: a refined architectural simplicity, solidity, and extreme cleanliness are admirable features of their temples. A wide central nave contains two ranks of stalls, whose enclosed pews are painted ash-grey, with seats and prayer rails covered in green velvet, each unfailingly furnished with a bible. Each stall has its owner. The two lateral naves also serve to support uncovered galleries, to which steps lead up rather like in an amphitheater. These are dedicated to those who don't own a

54 (*facing page, left*) William Kneass (after William Strickland), *Masonic Hall, Chestnut Street, Philadelphia*, 1813, engraving.

An early example of neo-Gothic architecture in the United States designed by its main protagonist, William Strickland.

55 (*above right*) John Hill (after Samuel Jones and John Lewis Krimmel), *The Burning of the Masonic Hall*, 1819, aquatint.

A major fire-fight such as this one on 9 March 1819 was a frenzied affair, but in this case the Hall was saved but for its tower and interior.

stall. The altar is meant to symbolize God and Nature, to whom they address their private devotions. The sound of a bell signals the time to assemble on the seventh day of each week. The first among them, be it man or woman, who feels inspired to speak, rises to his feet, bows to those around him, and utters these words: "Dearly beloved brothers and sisters, I have thought that in order to render greater glory to God and to best serve my neighbor that whatsoever course of action one might choose, though another one might do it in a different way or do nothing at all, I suggest to you that the most suitable solution . . .". And so forth and so on. Their thoughts are expressed with simple but effective eloquence, and always conclude with the exhortation: "If any among you finds me in error, or can think of a better way, I pray you to state it." Silence indicates approval. Otherwise another person rises, states his objections and adds his own opinion, always with the utmost mutual respect. Sometimes a whole session is spent in profound silence, and then the temple empties. The Lutherans never allow images of any sort (bad, very bad for the arts). A simple shrine serves as an altar. There they partake of the Holy Communion, which consists of a sliver of bread and a sip of wine. Their priest, or minister, is meant to have a wife and several times I saw him enter the church, arm in arm with his spouse. Then he would ascend to the pulpit to preach the Holy Gospel, instill high moral principles in his listeners, and intone praises to the Creator. They also have pew stalls, the only difference being that all the women group on the right, separated from the men who occupy the left-hand side. This and other similar sects pride themselves in having elaborate lamps distributed throughout their temples. They all profess the greatest civility toward strangers, immediately offering him a seat and a bible, as also happened to me often in Alsace. Their souls seem untroubled by doubts as to whether the stranger is a heretic or otherwise.

CEMETERIES   They greatly honor the memory of their ancestors and deceased relatives to the point, I would say, of worshipping their ashes. On Sundays, before and after mass, they visit the cemeteries behind the temple or parish church. They bring their children there to point out to them the inscriptions on the tombstones and the small plot of land that covers the remains of those who were their progenitors and benefactors. The mothers or adult relatives sometimes bring seeds or young shoots of aromatic herbs for the children to spread about or plant around the grave, while others festoon the tombs with garlands of flowers. Through these acts the practice of religion is born, and filial piety and veneration for their living elders is cultivated as well as a devout submission to the laws of nature. I never witnessed such a tender scene without feeling the deepest emotion in my heart.

OBSTACLES TO PASSING   Usually, as you know, one idea gives rise to another and a
UNDER THE EQUATOR   curiosity, once satisfied, will generate a new one. So as the time passed I was devising a plan to go to the place where people in the sunlight don't cast a shadow on the ground. I assure you that my curiosity was excited to the extreme, so eager was I to see the giant Boa raise himself up and work his way through the streets between the humble houses of the Carolinas, then creep inside to lap the food by the hearth and leave without harming any-

56   Benjamin Tanner (after John James Barralet), *Launch of the Steam Frigate Fulton the First at New York, 29 October 1814*, date unknown, aquatint.

In 1807 one observer described Fulton's first steamboat as "a sawmill on a raft and set afire," but by the time of Mauro's adventure elegant cabin accommodations were the order of the day.

one.[111] On the other hand, I would have been content to get to Havana, to visit our compatriot Gasparini as well as enjoy the chance to examine many specimens of natural history. So, eagerly inspired, I went down to the Port to find a boat, but heard from various captains that sinister rumors of a Yellow Fever epidemic in those parts were in the air, as well as reports of an inevitable insurrection of the Mexicans who were already troubling ships in the Gulf waters. Reflecting that prudence is the soul of good travelling, I abandoned the idea, and after fulfilling the duties of friendship, at dawn the following day I embarked on the steamboat to return to New York.

Steamboat   This marvellous invention of the American engineer Fulton is already too famous to allow of more than a brief mention.[112] The inventor, who was already quite wealthy, had by this time launched also a warship powered by steam. This prodigious phenomenon depends on the heat-generated expansion of water into vapor, an occurrence that the common housewife, never asking herself why, witnesses in the hole that our craftsmen make in their pan lids. This famous machine was not unknown to me, as I was perfectly aware of the fire pumps used in Paris.

The application, however, of the piston's motor power, with its movement up and down, causing the two huge wheels placed on the sides of the ship to function like oars, was truly worthy of a maritime genius. This vessel of huge proportions has three floors. The top deck is for promenading and is sheltered by awnings. The middle floor is divided into three areas, of which the central one houses the great furnace and the steam generator; the prow is for the convenience of the officers; and the stern is divided into two rooms, one for the men and the other for the women. The hold contains fuel and provisions. What I found uncomfortable was the deafening noise, and the jolts from the action of the pistons on the side-wheels. Aside from that, travelling by steamboat is quite convenient, faster, and more economical along the canals, navigable rivers, and even the sea. Going down the Delaware River one reaches the half-way point, little Elizabeth Town, where we found our four-horse coach ready. Passing through Brunswick, the second city of the state of New Jersey, we arrived in New York, having travelled over one hundred and fifty miles in less than a day, for the price of eight dollars.

FIRST CATHOLIC CHURCH IN NEW YORK

As I mentioned to you earlier, the Republican government of the United States tolerates the practice of all religious sects. Thus the Catholics of New York, eager to have their own church, sought financial help from their European friends and obtained it. Some Flemish bishops, being zealous propagators of the Holy Faith, sent them money, church furnishings, and three priests. The church is situated in the middle of a big field rather far from the city. It is of Gothic style, and instead of a painting over its single altar it has on the wall a frightful Calvary, painted by some Genoese in early July 1816, and this constitutes its sole ornamentation.[113] I had the satisfaction of being present at the opening of this temple, and attended the first solemn Mass that was celebrated there.[114] Here one is not dealing with the tyrannical oppression that forced the early Christians to hide in their catacombs. It is rather the burden of poverty that causes their churches to appear like larvae or embryos that will one day grow to colossal proportions, perhaps not inferior to those scattered under our beautiful Italian skies. I assure you that never before had I beheld a more vivid image of the early apostolic congregation of the faithful. Just one anecdote that I want to tell you will suffice to illustrate this. An organ, rather out of tune, struggled to play a confused and listless Kyrie Eleison, accompanied by three voices plus another. It sounded so odd to my ears that I could not resist my curiosity to see the singers. To do this, I had to climb up to a part of the orchestra separated from the center in the Flemish fashion, that is, surrounded by a dense choir screen. Heaving myself up as best I could on two wooden chairs, I managed to get a look at the singers. A woman stomped on the organ, making it screech, two little boys hesitantly stammered out a few notes, a young man sang the tenor line, and an old man muttered the bass part. The organist was struck by my curiosity and sent the tenor to invite me over. I accepted and greeted the lady in English, but since she affably replied in French, I reciprocated in kind. She asked me if I were from Paris, her own city, and when I answered that I was Italian she enthusiastically exclaimed, "Comment, Monsieur, Vous êtes Italian! Donc vous chanterez a nôtre place!" ("Why, Monsieur, you are Italian! So you will sing in our place!"), a frightening prospect, as if I had told her that I was Babini or Crivelli, but which nevertheless couldn't fail to arouse my pride in our harmonious nation. Happily for the good old man who was carrying the tune, I pleaded that a bad sore throat prevented me from obliging her request. I took note of her address, Mme Noo, who taught music and French as well. Promising to pay her a visit, I took my leave. The rest of the performance and the service itself proceeded in much the same way as the music. I shall say no more on the subject, except that two months later I saw, in Mr. Vecchio's shop, the oil painting of their titular Saint Patrick which had been donated to the church by the faithful citizens of Lille in Flanders.

NIAGARA   The summer season was rapidly drawing to a close. Winter, which according to the inhabitants begins in the autumn, pressed me to travel further north to visit a few lakes and the imposing Niagara Falls. By way of steamboat up the Hudson and stagecoach, I got to Albany, an unremarkable city of about eight thousand people, approximately one hundred and eighty miles from New York. A distance by road three times that long remained to reach Lakes Erie and Ontario. These should rather be called two fresh water seas. The Niagara river originates in the former, and before hurling itself into the latter it runs over submerged rocks and precipices with a roar that deafens the air itself. Once it reaches the edge of the cataracts, its breadth is estimated to measure eight hundred perches or thereabouts. This immense mass of water plunges from a height of twenty perches into the abyss, where it forms a violent turbulence and a foaming vortex, whose brilliance blinds the eye and whose thunder deafens the ear. Its roar can be heard fifty miles away. These falls, once seen, make all the others in the world seem like pygmies. From Lake Ontario rise the banks of the St Lawrence which passes through Quebec. But to be honest I was a bit dispirited by the rudeness of the inhabitants and the endless difficulties that I encountered en route, and I would be loathe to travel there ever again. On my return home I sought some much needed rest, surrounded by the attentions of my companion, and I could give myself over to completing some little tasks I had undertaken.

THEATER   Before you imagine me back in Europe, however, I don't want to deprive you of my observations on the subject of theater and music. I shall tell you that the first night I went to the theater the play was a tragedy entitled *Jane Shore*, and a musical by the title of *Killing No Murder*,[115] both of which occasioned the anticipated praise in their original English version. The interior is slightly larger than that of our demolished Marsigli Theater and is unique of its kind in New York.[116] It is built in the French fashion, with open galleries and no boxes, and with the fair sex excluded from the pit. The main actress, Mrs. Barnes,[117] was outstanding among the others for her personal beauty, her melodious voice, and clear diction, and for the nobility of her sentiments and acting which won her the love of the audience. So far as this went, the whole thing proceeded very well, and the audience, albeit generally cold in its response, did not stint its applause. But when it came to the farce, I swear to you that I

57 (*above*)   Nicolino Calyo, *The Bowery Boys*, c.1840, watercolor.

With their sidelocks soaped for swank effect, they lounged about the Bowery's low-class theaters when they were not scrapping with their rivals, the Dead Rabbits.

58 (*right*)   Anonymous, Broadsheet, *"Jane Shore"*, date unknown, letterpress.

"Jane Shore" was a popular play that underwent many variations throughout the century, its sentimental appeal based on the suffering of Edward IV's fictional mistress.

Booth's Theatre.

Lessees and Managers   Jarrett & Palmer

Third Week of the Triumphant
ENGAGEMENT OF

MISS GENEVIEVE WARD.

Final Representations in W. G. Wills's entirely new historical domestic play, of
Five Acts,

JANE SHORE!

Distribution of Characters:

DUKE OF GLOSTER.... .....Mr. GEORGE VANDENHOFF	
HENRY SHORE...............................Mr. MILNES LEVICK	
JOHN GRIST, a baker.................... ....Mr. JAS. H. TAYLOR	
LORD COOTES ....Mr. FRANK KILDAY	
CATESBY........ ....Mr. ANDREW JAQUES	
PRINCE EDWARD....... ....Miss BELLE WHARTON	
DUKE OF YORK....... ....Master WILLIE CARPENTER	
GRIM....... ....Mr. HENRY B. BRADLEY	
LAPRE........} Ruffians {.............Mr. JAMES STARK	
HEAD SERVANT ....Mr. WILLIAM RANOUS	
PETER TYLER ....} Tradesmen {.............Mr. JOHN BLAKE	
BILL COLE.......} {........Mr. JAMES FARRAR	
JANE SHORE ....MISS GENEVIEVE WARD	
QUEEN ELIZABETH ....KATE MEEK	
HOUSEKEEPER TO MRS. SHORE.................Madame I. C. MICHELS	
LADY COOTES.................................Miss JULIA VAUGHAN	
DAME GRIST................................Miss MARY WHARTON	
LADY MELLES.........................Miss FLORENCE GILLETTE	
LADY MELLON................................RETTA EDGERTON	

Lords, Ladies, Citizens, Soldiers, Ruffians, Beggars.
The piece produced under the immediate personal direction of GENEVIEVE WARD.

SYNOPSIS OF SCENERY.
ACT I.—A Chamber of State.
ACT II.—Shore's House.
ACT III.—Outer Hall, Crosby Palace.
ACT IV.—Charing Cross in Mid-Winter.
ACT V.—Shore's House.
The STAGE PAINTINGS, including the marvelous SNOW SCENS, are by MR.
CHARLES W. WITHAM.

ANNOUNCEMENT!
Next Monday, September 23d, Shakspere's

HENRY VIII.

Will be spectacularly produced, and on such a scale of grandeur that the magnificent panoply of HENRY V. and the Assyrian splendor of SARDANAPALUS will be far surpassed. GENEVIEVE WARD will appear as QUEEN KATHARINE.

59   John Searle, *Interior of the Park Theater, New York*, 1822, watercolor.

A prestigious theater that catered to upper-class clientele, but neither this representation nor Mauro's description conveys the audience's infamous rowdy behavior during the plays.

could have shed tears in favor of the tragedy, and I could have wept with chagrin at seeing how ruthlessly they ruined the music. To prove that I know whereof I speak, suffice it to say that the orchestra was formed of three violins, a horn, a clarinet, a viola, and a contrabass, but the last of these, which furnishes the indispensable harmonic base, was left lying aside by its owner. Highly irritated by this omission I began to ask some gentlemen, who appeared to possess some common sense, why on earth the conductor allowed such an important instrument to be neglected. One of them replied coldly, "Sir, this instrument is not really necessary." Pitying them, I turned my back on them. From my heart I invoked the memory of our Bolognese compatriots of whom I am bereft. I never set foot in the Theater again.

EXHIBITION ROOMS   An obligation had been felt to set up a fine arts exhibition: but to what end? Only, in my view, to do what everyone else did. Just behind the City Hall, a pretty good location, there was a building that they called the Academy, where some rooms, painted dark green, had been designated for the annual use of the above-mentioned exhibition.[118] The entrance ticket cost three quarters of a dollar.[119] I must begin by saying that Mr. Vanderlyn, on his return from his art studies in Paris, was among my circle of friends, and he graciously offered me a free ticket to the Academy. So I visited it, and I was pleased to observe at leisure a painting representing a sleeping Ariadne, and some good landscapes by the same Vanderlyn. I saw also several miniature portraits by a Monsieur Cola,[120] also very well-executed. However, though I remained for over an hour and a half, I saw only two visitors. "What does this absence of visitors mean?" I asked. "Do not be surprised," one of them replied, "It's because Ariadne is nude."[121] I bade "Good Day" to those gentlemen, "A cui si fa notte innanzi sera!" ("To those who walk in darkness though the evening has scarce begun").

The young Vanderlyn was in a bad mood over this incident, but being also carried away by the national spirit of speculation, he showed me a pencil portrait of Monroe, the new presidential candidate, for me to engrave with the understanding that we'd share the profits equally. But since I was determined to return among people who are not repelled by the sight of the Creator's masterwork as He had made it (considered here such a scandal), I declined the proposition, and persuaded him to offer it to my friend Gimbrede instead. As it turned out, this was to be a very favorable arrangement for my friend, as the subject represented was indeed elected to the Presidency.[122]

WOOD ENGRAVINGS

On the subject of engraving, justice requires me to tell you that New York is proud to claim good old Anderson, an admirable wood engraver not inferior to Branson of London in engraving on boxwood.[123] He has a little shop at the beginning of the Bowery which also serves as his studio. He presented me with two collections. The first was a whole Bible, the second consisted of thirty-eight illustrations for the Works of Shakespeare. These are outstanding for their technical precision. I was also given a proof impression of siderography (now in current use), invented by Mr. Perkins (an American),[124] and several impressions of stereotypes, with corrections from the foundry of the Quaker Mr. Collins whom I mentioned above.

THE CONSTITUTION AT RISK

Already at that time there were rumblings about whether it would be beneficial to cancel the article of their Constitution that prohibited wars of aggression or any other hostile measure under whatever political objective. The dedicated enforcers of the Constitution, those of a more delicate sensibility, were opposed to this cancellation. Those eager to expand, and the emissaries of England, were in favor, even though it was wrong in principle, and appealed to Monroe, he being of the same opinion as the case of the Two Floridas demonstrated later. I can't help but tell you that in my opinion, seeds of destruction were sown by this. Just as the Roman Republic and even the Empire itself were annihilated in similar ways, so this nascent colossus will either shorten its own existence, or it will succumb under the weight of its own expansion.[125]

EMBARCATION: DEPARTURE FROM AMERICA

And so I yielded to an impulse whose cause I did not know to see once more my native land. And since I as a stranger would be leaving behind some friends who appreciated my humble talents, at home I would be doubly compensated by the sweetness of old friendship and the boundless resources of my *patria*. I therefore went to the port and contracted for passage on a ship that was to set sail in September for Havre-de-Grace. On returning home I met young William Main[126] accompanied by some other people. I should clarify that this American, an engraving enthusiast, was constantly visiting me. Since I had persuaded him that Italy is truly the mistress who nourishes the liberal arts, he had induced several of his friends to provide him with an allowance of a dollar a day for three years, as long as I agreed to take him with me and to instruct him. To this they consented. One of his brothers was the accountant of the rich Graham, who owned some large ships including the magnificent Trident weighing 800 tonnes, which was to set sail in August for Gibraltar, Leghorn, and then Calcutta in the Indies. Accordingly William could have free passage on this vessel. He nearly died of sorrow when he heard that I had already arranged to see Paris again and then return to Italy. But he went to such great lengths to persuade me that I yielded to his requests in order to please these gentlemen. So they offered me a new contract by which they reimbursed me for the fifty dollars that I had paid down as a deposit, and furthermore obligated themselves to pay my travelling expenses and those of my lady for the journey, including our stay in Gibraltar.

I resolved to accept the offer on account of the most pleasant prospect of setting foot in Africa, not that I knew the least thing about Spanish customs and despite my aversion to travelling in the Mediterranean. The arrangement, which included lodgings and passage with meals at the table of Captain Rae, was to cost merely three hundred and fifty dollars for the two of us. The other passengers made for excellent company. They included the Swedish Consul Bergins (for whom I later wrote a letter of introduction to Madame Martinetti, when I was in Florence), some English people, and businessmen from Gibralter such as Mr. Allison, Mr. Angli, and others. We entertained ourselves by playing music, or exchanging curious and instructive andecdotes, and so we passed the time most agreeably. The only disturbing character was an old Dalmatian scoundrel, a failed privateer captain who came very near to getting thrown overboard to feed the fish.

Fishing for the Horseshoe Crab

On the third day of our journey I noticed a certain creature surfacing close by that was definitely not a turtle, and I begged the Captain to let me have some fishing tackle. And although his manners were rough and brusque, as is usual with sailors, he was not so discourteous as to deny my request. The enterprise entailed no little effort as it was necessary to lower the lifeboat with four or six men, cast off from the ship, and row toward the fish whereas the ship itself travelled at fifteen miles an hour. But by diligent effort and a few dollars at hand, one can overcome all obstacles. I hauled in a Horseshoe Crab, or the King of Crabs, also known as the Poliphemus of the Ocean.[127] It was three or four times larger than the specimens displayed in the science cabinets of Paris and Florence, nor is there a specimen in the cabinet in Pavia, or in many others. I was thus highly pleased to donate it in homage to our own Institute, which also lacked an example. It is equipped with a long tail, solid, triangular, and pointed. It hunts oysters and other bivalves. It lies in ambush, and when one of these opens up, it quickly pierces the gaping shell with the point of its tail, then brings the oyster to its mouth and sucks out the tiny creature.

SEA SWALLOWS   Among the many remarkable things that I came across during my pleasant journey, I'd like to call your attention to various species of birds that never leave the surface of the sea. The swallow, for instance, since it isn't good to eat, reproduces in great numbers. It is a web-footed bird, and it feeds on small fish. How does it build a nest? And how does it hatch its eggs, you may ask? Why, under its own wings, taking turns in its maternal duties with its mate.[128]

FLYING FISH   The flying fish, once believed to be imaginary creatures, do in fact exist. I observed whole schools of them, and I even held one in my own hands. Their dorsal fins expand and are similar to the wings of the insect that we commonly call the dragonfly. They leap out of the water and fly all together above the waves, until the moisture on their bodies has dried off, and if they happen to fly right beneath the sun rays, across from the observer, the shimmering reflections are marvellous to behold.

REMEDY AGAINST SEASICKNESS   As we came within sight of the Azores, we were caught in such a violent storm that few of us escaped seasickness. Teresa remained unaffected by it, but thanks to my own foolhardiness, I very nearly threw up. However, when I retreated to our quarters and lay down in the lavatory, I managed to avoid it.[129] I must tell you that this experience taught me that there is no better preventive measure for this sickness than lying down, and here is how I found this out. Once while travelling on a little fishing boat from Venice to Ancona on my way to Rome, a terrible storm at sea assailed us. Because this rough old boat had no comfortable living quarters, I was forced to take shelter inside a makeshift storeroom closed off from the deck. Not even the sailors remained unaffected by the seasickness, and on this occasion when once the danger had passed and they realized that I had not suffered at all, they marvelled. I have given the subject some thought since. From the experience I had, I have gathered that this malaise is provoked by a number of factors. First of all I believe that nausea is produced by the undulation of the vessel, which disturbs the peristaltic motions of the intestines. This stimulates the diaphragm, which in turn presses against the stomach, which subsequently seeks to empty itself by violent spasms. Secondly, the stench of the sea water, especially when it is agitated, is enough to bring on a violent queasiness in the nervous system and the stomach. Last but not least, I firmly believe that ones imagination becomes over-active at the sight of danger and so many things upside down, and that this contributes a great deal to the indisposition. Assuming then that by lying down the conflicting movements are reduced eighty percent, and that by staying indoors neither the senses of sight or smell will receive unpleasant stimulation, one concludes that as a consequence one remains unscathed by seasickness. This was indeed proved by people who tested my system. I wish that those more knowledgeable than myself would look into this matter, and that by way of authoritative evidence render a useful service to mankind. The fumes from strong acids were once believed to be an excellent antidote to seasickness, but in the end it doesn't work. A common prejudice prevails among sailors, the belief, that is, that one feels better by staying on the deck. The facts confute this, since the malaise does not spare them although in my view they are amphibious animals.

THE CHICKENS ARE MADE TO SUFFER FROM THIRST   Another remarkable custom that prevailed among the crew was that of not allowing the chickens and the livestock to drink. Consequently these creatures were driven mad with thirst, and got so dehydrated that we felt as though we were eating wood instead of meat. I pitied those poor humans who, accustomed since childhood to eating salted meat, preferred a drop of verminous water to a good chicken. As for us, however, we managed to keep some of these birds well provided with water and made of them a fine feast.

FEAR OF THUNDERBOLTS

One day, as the clouds gathered densely above us, we feared, not without good reason, to be struck by lightning. Especially dangerous were the three huge anchors, with their long, pointed ends. But the skillful Captain speedily arranged for the spare anchor to be hoisted as a lightning rod, and after the long iron chain was released in the sea we were saved once again.

WATERSPOUT

The penultimate serious danger to which our ship was subjected was the waterspout, which raced in our pursuit following a thunderstorm. In truth, only a Galileo or a Newton could possibly explain this phenomenon and not I. Whatever kind of chemical laboratory is up there in the sky? But confident of the indulgence you bear toward me, I'll tell you as much as I do know. This is the deadliest of all phenomena for those who travel by sea. Should it ever strike, total destruction is inevitable. So far as I have been able to comprehend, it is generated by a fierce whirlwind that gathers a vast quantity of sea water up into itself, wrapping around it until it forms a wide, dense column issuing from the clouds, and sometimes actually joining the sea to the clouds. In this case the ship sinks, spinning down into the cavity produced by the vortex. There are times when an ancient oak tree is uprooted by the strength of a hurricane, and in like manner a ship can be tossed into the air. What a terrifying nautical flight! It is customary, on sighting a waterspout, to shoot off the cannons but this is not always effective in dissipating it.

TURTLE DOVE

As we progressed in our journey a lovely turtledove came to rest on the top-most yard of the main mast. You can imagine how overjoyed the entire crew was at the sight, and the First Mate would have been misled, if his precise sea maps hadn't confirmed that we were still 1,500 miles away from the nearest coast. Therefore this bird must have flown on the wings of the wind two whole days and two nights, presumably at the speed of thirty miles an hour! Indeed it was so exhausted that it let one of the sailors hold it in his hand.

Behold! There before our very eyes lay two worlds, Africa and Europe. On our right stood the Atlas Mountains, competing in stature with the Mountains of the Moon; and there was Tenerife and the city of Tangiers of the Moroccan Empire. On our left, the impregnable city and fortress of Gibraltar, once a Moorish territory, then Spanish, and nowadays English. The strait is three leagues wide and eight long, and through it flows the Atlantic waters into the Mediterranean, aided by the winds that favor their passage. An indentation of the coastline forms the bay and the safe port of Gibraltar that looks toward the west. This is one of the busiest harbors in the world, thanks to its central location. It is a free port, and there would be no more seductive place on earth, if it weren't subject to epidemics of the plague. This formidable rock rises 1,700 feet above sea level (in English measurement) and those who can afford it pitch their tents and sleep up there when the nights are hot. It is joined to the Spanish continent by a low tongue of land on the north. As far as I could ascertain, the cliff is formed of a friable quartz rock, and is therefore quite barren and unwelcoming although favorable to such succulent plants as aloe, agave, cactus, mesembryanthemum (a kind of marigold), and others, which grow here to a stunning height. Somehow, being industrious, they have devised ways to cultivate vines, citrus trees, and other such plants which embellish their hanging gardens.

The city is almost at sea level and has only one long street which is very dusty. There are about six thousand residents, counting among them people from all nations, although the majority are Spanish. The merchants in oriental costume that congregate there offer a superb contrast to the various different forms of dress of the other nations. There was a Spanish church of the Servite order and another for the various sects tolerated by the English regime. The southern end of the street led to some well-cultivated stretches of sandy soil. Further along one comes across some attractive barracks and the military hospital of the garrison. Finally one arrives at the lowest part, the tip of the rock (in antiquity called Finis Terrae). There the impregnable fortress was planted that guards and defends the entrance to the strait on the east and the west sides. One might well say that it is easier to reach the watery globe of the moon than to conquer this site. Inlets were conspicuous, their little streams of water skimming along in all directions, a new sight for me. Innumerable small forts, carved out of the rock itself, were scattered along all the sides of the isolated island that look toward the mainland. As I went, or rather clambered, up to observe some of these (from a due distance), I took the opportunity to get someone to lower me into the so-called cellar of St. Michael, where the waters that seeped through from the top form large stalactites and stalagmites of different shapes, resembling grotesque figures and large pillars. A particular type of monkey originally from Africa, known as the macaque, adjusted to this country and multiplied remarkably.

AFRICA

One fine morning, the sea being calm, I had them transport me in a big rowboat to the shore on the other side of the strait, and setting foot on land I said to myself: "Here I am in Africa, in the kingdom of Morocco, right at the edge of Tangiers." Woe betide me if Captain Rae had found me out, since ships coming from the waters off Gibraltar are suspect in the eye of many governments, and especially dreaded are those whose passengers have touched ashore on the coasts of Africa, which is constantly affected by epidemics of disease. And because my escapade was clandestine and I wasn't carrying the necessary passport, I had to keep my visit short. I observed in the distance the buildings of the city, and the outlines of houses and mosques, which were built in an architectural style altogether too baroque to merit the slightest attention. I picked the fruits of a *chenin dactilifera*, a cane of *suarum officinalis*, and of a *cercis silaguastrum*.[130] I also collected several seeds from plants considered exotic in our country, and even gathered a fair quantity of sand, the same kind of sand that, driven by the wind in the desert, envelopes entire caravans, burying them alive.

ENGLISH FLEET

On returning to Gibraltar, I was fortunate enough to witness the English fleet's return to port after the siege of Algeria. The garrison obliged to do the honors for Admiral Exmouth sent down a directive to the Captains of all the ships at anchor recommending that the passengers remain on board, and I was advised to stay on board with the other spectators.

For brevity's sake here I shall skip over the displays of military manoeuvres so that you may participate vicariously for a moment in the last artillery volley. A signal was given simultaneously to all the cannoneers, and six hundred and forty cannons blasted out one thunderous volley. The entire rock was ablaze. The earth, air, and the sea itself were violently convulsed. We were left stunned, confounded, and deprived of our senses. It would be impossible to witness such a rare spectacle anywhere else in the world, except in this same place and in identical circumstances. To conclude, I shall tell you that the reverberations between the mountains of Africa and those of Spain lasted for a whole half hour, to our universal amazement.

But there would be no reward in picking roses if they didn't come with thorns. And so it happened that on the last evening of our ten-day stay in Gibraltar, thanks to my recklessness, I ran the risk, along with my companion, of becoming the victim of two Italian jailbirds. At sunset the gates to the city would close, and by special concession of Commandante La Piazza there was a half an hour period during which we were allowed to enter and leave through a small gate leading to the little tongue of land I described above. When we discovered that we were late, we only just managed to obtain permission to exit, since we did not intend to spend the night off the ship. The distance to the port was considerable. But then, having noticed a row boat on the beach, I walked up and contracted to be transported to the Trident by the two sailors who owned it. It didn't take me long to realize that they were heading in a direction diametrically opposed to the right one, but they took no notice of my lively protestestations. Some words in Neapolitan dialect escaped them, which further confirmed my fears that they intended to drown us, under cover of darkness, in the depths of the bay surrounded by deserted land. I swiftly pushed my companion aside and leapt furiously to my feet, my two pistols in hand. I braced one against my chest, and with my left hand I grabbed hold of the boat's little rudder. I cried out that these traitors would face the death penalty if they did not turn around at once, or at least stop rowing with all their might in the wrong direction. They muttered "*Ah, bene mio*, by San Gennaro!", and other similarly crude expressions, but they obeyed. This dreadful situation was worsened still by the danger of being submerged by the waves that a violent wind had called up. Finally, thank Heavens, we arrived within calling distance of our Captain on the ship, and we warned him not to let the two villains come on board. Following my report of the events, he was determined to have them chained and consigned to the severe Maritime Tribunal for judgment, and only acceded to our heated supplications to the contrary so that our departure wouldn't be delayed by a trial. So, the two were chased off in disgrace.

On the 15th of September the sails were once again unfurled. It was expedient to sail along the coast of Spain, and this was accomplished without any serious risk.

But as we came in sight of of the Island of Corsica we ran into a fierce danger, right on the last night of our trip. A furious wind off the land was blowing us irresistibly toward the rock of Gorgogne, despite the fact that the ship was drawing nineteen feet and the sails had been furled. I was awakened by the creaking of the ship and by the desperate cries of the entire crew. We were running so strongly to windward that only by clutching, like a cat, at the furniture and the trunks, all of which were in great disarray, did I manage to struggle to a point where I could see the circles of light cast by the hanging lamp that was lurching precariously, and realized that the floor of our quarters was thirty five degrees off the horizontal.

To be shattered and drowned, this was the fate that awaited us after so many narrow escapes from death, when our brave Captain, outdoing himself and exceeding the normal procedures, suddenly seized the horns of the dilemma and flew up to the quarter-deck. As we would say where we come from, "to be crushed by either its teeth or its jaws," and he ordered, to the amazement of the crew, that the great lateen sail be hoisted.

DEPARTURE FROM GIBRALTAR

DANGER OF SHIPWRECK AGAINST ROCKS

BRAVERY OF CAPTAIN RAE

Recourse to such strategy pushed our ill-fated situation to its limits, but the result proved that sometimes one poison is an antidote to another one much worse, and so the ship, along with our friend, was saved. This expedient was put on the record, and it has since served to improve the techniques of navigation, to the credit of the American genius.

PORT OF LEGHORN   In spite of the equinox, we dropped anchor at the port of Leghorn on the 24th of September, after travelling eight hundred and twenty two miles on the Mediterranean.[131] Adding to this distance the outbound journey and the return, plus six hundred around the coast of America and the sixty between Leghorn and Florence, our trip covered over nine thousand nine hundred miles. It has cost 12,796 lire for the two of us, and we had cut a fine figure everywhere we went.

LAZZARETTO OF   In the early morning, in a cheerful frame of mind, we all put
S. GIACOMO   on our best clothes as a sign of respect towards our flag and lined up on the deck to await the medical inspection. Although, thank God, we were all in good health, nevertheless *ad cautelam* we had to pass a half-quarantine in the public hospital. I confess that I was not in the least displeased by this obligatory break in the journey, for various reasons. One was that I needed to refresh my eyes, worn out by the hydrogen gas and phosphorescent light that the waves sprayed up as they broke against the ship at night. The other was to gain an understanding of the institutional functioning of a quarantine station, and to observe at first hand the domestic customs of the individuals of different nationalities who were detained there. As a special favor I obtained a clean and separate room for just the two of us. One proviso was exacted, however, that the whole company would feel free to call upon the good services of my companion in order to pass the dinner hour more agreeably.[132]

I believe that a single incident will suffice to give you a clear idea of the austere regime of such places. A party of Armenian Israelites appeared the thirty-ninth day of the quarantine. At one point a young boy who was looking out of a window dropped his cap down onto the ground of the little piazza. One of the above mentioned Hebrews, who resided in a different dormitory, picked it up and tossed it back up to the boy. A guard saw this and reproached him for this action, whereupon the poor Israelite suffered the misery of watching his friends depart while he had to begin his quarantine all over again. Such severity didn't spare even the most eminent people on earth, and the only alternative was to spend the requisite period of time on board the ship that had brought us to port. To share a pinch of tobacco, its box would be placed on the ground, then the person offering it would step away, and finally he would take back the box when the other had finished. If, while taking a walk, a flap of your clothes should touch those of someone from a different family, you had to start the quarantine all over again, free of any suspect contact until the prescribed period had passed.

CONCLUSIONS

Thus, my dearest friend, I conclude my feeble sketch of this most pleasant journey. And if ever anyone should ask you what I gained, or saw, or learned, or obtained, or even how I matured in the course of my travels, pray tell him in my name that I have acquired the treasure of objectivity, an understanding of the relationships between the diverse ways that men think, and the richness of spirit through which we are able to overcome those very passions that are most wearisome and excruciating, by this I mean to say our opinions.

What did I see?

An infinite array of wonderful things that inspired me anew to honor the Deity through the nature of things in themselves, while at the same time the spectacle of these miracles has humbled my pride.

What did I learn?

Not only have I learned, but indeed experienced for myself that the honest, industrious, and courageous man is a citizen of the world.

What did I gain?

That by decisive action and sobering example, I have perhaps rendered a service to other unfortunate fathers and husbands.

What did I attain?

That, satiated with the bounties of the world, I can die content.

Keep well, and God be with you.

Notes

All references to "Lettere" refer to Gandolfi, Mauro, "Lettere," Biblioteca comunale dell'Archiginnasio di Bologna, Autografi raccolti da Ciprano Pallotti e da lui legatati al Municipio di Bologna, vol. XIV, 6, nos. 815–81.

Introduction

1 Teresa Diani was a thirty-five-year-old widow when she joined Mauro for the voyage. She lived with him until 1828, although he discreetly referred to her as his "governante," or housekeeper throughout the manuscript. It is likely that this little subterfuge was intended to shield him, in the event of the manuscript's being published, from further accusations of immorality.

2 In March 1817 one traveller recorded that the steerage passage from Ireland was £14 which included a weekly allotment of beef, biscuits, soup, flour, water, and cooking privileges (Palmer, 1818, p. 1).

3 Mauro's description of the journey's duration and its captain is confirmed by an entry in New York's *Commercial Advertiser* of 18 May 1816. Its "Ships' Listing" notes that there "arrived last evening the Brigadier William and Henry," with a Captain Almy in command. This information also appeared in the *New York Gazette* (New York Historical Society Library, Periodical Collections), under "General Advertiser."

4 The manuscript forms part of the Collezioni d'arte e di storia of the Cassa di Risparmio in Bologna (Fondazione Carisbo, Fondo Ambrosini 4507.CIII.op.52), which has kindly given me permission to publish it. The daily passenger lists do not mention Mauro and Teresa, nor are they listed in Filby and Meyer, 1981.

5 Frances Trollope, *The Domestic Manners of the Americans*, 1832, and Charles Dickens, *American Notes*, 1842. Another traveller in 1817 had this to say: "Most of the travels I have seen are full of prejudice and invective against the Americans, which in some instances the authors could scarcely feel" (Palmer, 1818, p. 2).

6 *Luigi Castiglione's Viaggio: Travels in the United States of North America 1785–1787.* Translated and edited by Antonio Pace, Syracuse, 1983.

7 Gualandi was acquainted with the Gandolfi family, though I could find no discussion of his project to transcribe the "Voyage" manuscript in the thirty-nine letters he exchanged with another of Mauro's friends, the painter Pelagio Palagi, dating from the 1830s on, in the Biblioteca Comunale of the Archiginnasio in Bologna. There is a mention of Mauro's little brother Protasio in a letter from Palagi to Gualandi of 13 March 1836 (Carteggio Palagi, lettere al fratello Giuseppe, Michelangelo Gualandi, ed altri, Biblioteca Comunale dell'Archiginnasio di Bologna, Autografi raccolti da Ciprano Pallotti e da lui legatati al Municipio di Bologna, vol. XXIV, no. 1440.

8   Scarabelli, 1842. The following year Scarabelli published his essay on Mauro (Scarabelli, 1843).

9   Dr. Zanotti comments: "The 'Voyage to America,' written in June 1822, of which I hold the original manuscript signed with a simple 'MG,' had come down to me as inheritance with other of his writings and drawings . . . What he tells of the life he lived abroad, the various people he knew, the artists he cited, and the works of art he made outside of his native land allows us to familiarize ourselves a bit with the ambience and the customs of other people. It is thus of major importance for those times, and of interest as well for our fellow citizens" (Zanotti, 1925, pp. 73–4). The translations of all quotations other than the *Journey* are my own.

10   The story of the destruction of the papers was told to me in 1979 by one of Dr. Zanotti's descendants. The Allied bombing campaign carried out in the summer and autumn of 1944 had focused on Bologna because it was strategically located on the via Emilia, the main road since Roman times from Rome to Milan. It was also a critical north–south and east–west railroad terminal (Goldoni et al., 1980, section 19).

11   In one section, however, Mauro notes that he was responding to questions that the "friend" had asked concerning the summer climate of New York compared with that of Milan.

12   There was a large influx of these French speaking people, and to New York alone it is estimated that by the end of 1793 some four to five thousand had immigrated. Mrs. Logan noted that in Philadelphia "Great numbers of French men, now in their turn fleeing from proscription, have lately arrived on our shores. Among them is Joseph Buonaparte who figured a short time under his brother's protection" (Logan, 1816–17, p. 2). See also Burrows and Wallace, 1999, p. 313.

13   The "Stati delle anime" are church census records listed by address and furnish ages and birth dates of all residents. The years with which we are concerned are intact for the parish of Sta. Maria Maddalena. Mauro's name is first recorded as living at the Casa Palotti in 1766 at age two. His name disappeared in 1782, reappeared in 1787, and is absent permanently after 1789, thus confirming the dates of other accounts. The house was directly across the street from the present Pinacoteca Nazionale di Belle Arti but was destroyed in the Second World War. His sister and brothers are recorded as follows: Damiano I, born in 1766 but died in infancy; Damiano II, born in 1769; Marta, born in 1771; Protasio, born in 1774; Martino, born in 1777; and Emidio, born in 1780.

14   The autobiography, written in 1833, was published exactly as Mauro had written it and Zanotti added his own commentaries as footnotes (Zanotti, 1925). It was also published in a very few copies in 1840 by the Milanese publishers Pietro and Giuseppe Vallardi as a pamphlet entitled *Non ti scordar di me*. I could find no copies of this.

15   Zanotti, 1925, p. 75.

16   Zanotti, 1925, p. 75. Mauro's close copies after not only Gaetano's but also Ubaldo's drawings confound scholars to this day (Cazort, 1995).

17   Zanotti, 1925, pp. 76–7. Mauro claimed he was only sixteen when he made this dramatic decision, a fact discounted by documentation, but perpetuated by later

writers. His adventures in France were verified at the time of his marriage to Laura Zanetti in 1792 by the Bolognese authorities who were obliged to check out his story in order to remove any suspicions of bigamy. Mauro's name was cleared, and the resulting legal document allows us to establish that he was absent from Bologna from July 1782 to October 1787 (Bagni, 1992, p. 469, n. 19).

18 Scarabelli, 1843. Scarabelli seems to have drawn heavily on Mauro's autobiography for his facts.

19 The seasick remedy is told differently in the "Voyage," see p. 110.

20 Zanotti, 1925, p. 77.

21 Bagni, 1992, p. 468, n. 6 (quoting Archivi Nazionale di Bologna, the lawyer Francesco Triboli, 1783, "mazzo 5,8,9, f.24"), and n. 7.

22 Zanotti, 1925, pp. 78–9, n. 18. Carlo Caprara, member of an old aristocratic Bolognese family and son of Nicoló Caprara Montecuccoli, was one of the two senators elected in May 1796 to negotiate with the approaching French. Although they did not deal directly with Napoleon, they succeeded in conveying the determination of the Bolognese to be independent. Napoleon promised autonomy to the Senate, a move which turned out to be manipulatory. Caprara was later an active member of the Cisalpine Republican government and accepted the grandiose title granted by Napoleon of Great Keeper of the Shield (Cavazza, 1978, p. 302).

23 Zanotti, 1925, p. 7; Scarabelli, 1843, p. 9. See Rosenberg and Sebastiani, 1977; and Cazort, 1993a. These carriages are currently at the Musée des Voitures in Compiègne. Restored in the 1950s, their pristine condition is also due to the fact that they were used only ceremonially. Count Caprara was elected Gonfaloniere in 1790, a ceremonial post soon to be terminated by Napoleon's cancellation of noble titles. The carriages and processions are shown in some of the miniature illustrations, or *insigne*, in the Insignia deglianziani del comune 1580–1796, Archivio di Stato, Bologna, vol. 15, cc.174b–175a.

24 Rosenberg and Sebastiani, 1977, pp. 240–41, repr. The Tanari family had been among Gaetano's early patrons, and it was probably his connections that procured the commission for Mauro.

25 The "Atti e memorie dell' Accademia Clementina," the fascinating records of the Academy's meetings, show that it also arranged assistance for widows and orphans of deceased artists and, if they had died on the job, of transferring the commissions to another artist in their ranks. The "Atti" manuscripts are held by the current Accademia delle Belle Arti. The Clementina was renowned throughout Italy for its instruction in figure drawing, and a number of prominent eighteenth-century Venetian artists including Sebastiano Ricci and Giambattista Piazzetta came to Bologna for study.

26 See Cazort, 1979, nos. 306–7, pls. 305–6; and Cazort, 1993b, no. 111.

27 "Libro dei matrimoni 1792," Parish of S. Benedetto, Bologna.

28 Zanotti, 1925, p. 79.

29 This information comes from Zanotti, 1925, pp. 79–80, n. 22. Curiously, Mauro never mentioned this son's name in his various writings.

30 Clementina (1795–1848) was married in 1815 to a printer, Giuseppe Grassili. Widowed, she was married again in 1841 to

Onofrio Zanotti, a painter and quadratur-ist (artists who produced the elaborate illu-sionistic fresco surrounds for the Bolognese wall and ceiling decorations). She was a musician and watercolorist, and in 1837 was elected to the Accademia, by then called the Accademia delle Belle Arti. It was she who assembled the family papers that her great-grandson Dr. Zanotti used as the basis for his publica-tions on the Gandolfi.

31   Zanotti, 1925, p. 81.

32   The identification of the portrait as being of Mauro was originally owing to a sug-gestion by Francesco Archangeli (oral communication in 1967 to the present writer from its owner, Francesco Molinari Pradelli). The identification of the subject is borne out by a feature-by-feature com-parison with the *Self Portrait with Guitar and Palette*. This method of subject identi-fication, which entails a precise measure-ment of distances between critical points of feature as a means of establishing likenesses beween two faces seen from different points of view, was developed by the staff of the Criminal Identification Unit of the Royal Canadian Mounted Police, to whom I am grateful for this assistance.

33   Volpe, 1979, p. 125, no. 257 as by Gaetano and possibly representing "The face of the Jacobin and adventurous Mauro," whose allegiance to the revolutionary elements in Bologna are frequently referred to in early biographies.

34   Emliani, 1967, pp. 413–4; Roli, 1977, pp. 176, 130, 265; Volpe, 1979, p. 141, pl. 302. The painting was transferred, along with other self-portraits by the academicians, to the Accademia di Belle Arti at the time of its formation in 1804. A copy of the por-trait in brown wash by Clementina is cur-rently in the Archiginnasio di Bologna (Zanotti, 1925, p. 75, repr.).

35   "Atti e Memorie dell' Accademia Clementina," MS LV, cc.331–2 and 404–5, Accademia delle Belle Arti, Bologna.

36   Zanotti, 1925, p. 149.

37   Riccomini, 1971, no. 92.

38   Bagni, 1992, p. 478, no. 449.

39   Bagni, 1992, p. 477, no. 448.

40   The painting and drawing are currently attributed to Gaetano. Bagni (1992, nos. 275–8), cites as reference Luigi Tonini, 1864, p. 31. Tonini's guide book to Rimini, the earliest reference to the painting, includes the painting in his Index as "Mauro," who is clearly the author of the drawing.

41   Luciano Guerzoni, "Il mondo delle Opere pie," in Bentini et al., 1980, pp. 13–22; Cazort and Johnson, 1982, pp. 16–17.

42   Zanotti, 1925, pp. 151–3. Mauro's vivid descriptions of the early days of French occupation and the growing disillusion-ment of the local Jacobin sympathizers deserves translation and publication.

43   Orioli, 1903 (n.p.); Zanotti, 1925, p. 146. Even the sober chronicler Guidicini waxed eloquent over the event: "The whole Piazza was illuminated, and there were two orchestras there, one composed of violins, basses and contrabasses, the other the of the numerous bands of the civic guard, including some singers." (Guidicini, 1886–7, p. vii)

44   Orioli, 1903 (n.p.).

45   His design was officially approved at the meeting in Ferrara of the *Giunta di Difesa Generale* on 11 November 1796. The flag, and even its flagpole, is described in detail in a note from "cittadino Mauro Gandolfi" to "cittadino Carlo Caprara." The banner

was to be made of silk, 6.5 × 5.5 Bolognese feet in three horizontal rows: green at the bottom, white in the middle, and red at the top. The white band, the largest, will show the fasces, oak branch, and Phrygian cap of the Republic with appropriate letters in gold on the other bands (Zanotti, 1925, p. 74; Zanotti, 1941, pp. 6–7; Orioli, 1903; and "La Storia del tricolore italiano," 1907.

46 I am grateful to Alan Stone and Leslie Hill for this information.

47 Zanotti, 1925, p. 146; Scarabelli, pp. 10–11.

48 Zecchi, 1828, p. xxxiv.

49 Mauro's project for the "Cimetero Monumentale" existed as late as 1925 in the Archivio di Stato in Bologna (Zanotti, 1925, p. 146, n. 33).

50 "And when Napoleon wished two crowns on his August forehead, and bequeathed the beautiful name of Italy to one of his kings, there was little hope for the unity of our country, because it didn't even have its own boundaries" (Guidicini, 1886–7, p. vii).

51 Zanotti, 1925, p. 145 and n. 29. The Congress rotated its meeting sites between Modena, Bologna, Ferrara, and Reggio Emilia.

52 Local resentment smouldered, and in 1831 a revolt began in Modena and spread through Emilia-Romagna. Bologna was briefly proclaimed "Stato delle provincie unite," but the Austrian troops put an end to the unrest. Mauro stated in one of his letters that his youngest brother Emidio was active in the uprising.

53 "Libro dei matrimoni," 23 September 1795, parish of Sta. Maria Maddalena, the parish of Mauro's parents. In the eulogy that Democrito delivered on the first anniversary of his father's death, he said that his mother Caterina came from Catania to Bologna with her father, a dancing teacher, had married for love, and was young and very beautiful (she was twenty-seven), but had never lived with his father (Zanotti, 1925, p. 76, n. 9).

54 Letter to the Judge of the Peace, Tribunal of Reno, 30 September 1798. Cited in Bagni, 1992, pp. 470–71, and n. 34. The legal dissolution of the marriage did not occur at that time. In a later letter to the judicial magistrate in Milan, "Sig. Auditore Ugolino," Mauro recalls their earlier collaboration in May 1809 to work out the terms of a divorce decree ("Lettere," 29 September 1821).

55 Farneti, 1988, p. 129.

56 Letter to a fellow artist, Francesco Rosaspina, 29 March 1798 (cited in Bagni, 1992, p. 470, n. 33 as being in the Biblioteca Comunale di Forlì, Raccolta Piancastelli, Sezione Autografi, a.n.).

57 "To Mauro Gandolfi, an annual subsidy of eight hundred forty milanese lire to relocate in Paris in order to perfect his skills in the graphic arts" (Archivio Dipartimentale del Reno, Istruzione Pubblica, vol. 2, n. 736, allegato n. 2, cited in Bagni, p. 471, n. 39). From this subsidy guaranteed by the Institute Mauro had to deduct his payment to Caterina.

58 McKee, 1993, p. 2.

59 McKee, 1993, p. 4.

60 Scarabelli listed forty prints by Mauro, including a single item described as, "32 vignette allusive alla D.zia," evidently a reference to his ephemeral etchings "alluding to democracy." These prints have never been itemized but are recognizable by their distinctive style and often the inclusion of his distinctive cursive initials. More prints can be found in the New York Public

Library, the Fogg Museum, and the Philadelphia Museum of Art (see Apell, 1880, for the basic listing). Mauro began to sign and date his prints only after his return from America, and then only sporadically. He specified eighteen prints in his *testamento* that he wanted to leave to "Sig. Giovanni Zecchi, negoziante e stampatore," a dealer, printer, and author of the account of the Certosa cemetery mentioned above.

61   "Protocollo Riservato di Legazione," 3 January 1815, n. 8. These details are told with relish and documentation by Dr. Zanotti in his annotations to Mauro's autobiography (Zanotti, 1925, p. 76, n. 9 and p. 379, n. 74).

62   Scarabelli, 1843, p. 14. For a discussion of collecting specimens of natural history at this time with its emphasis on classification systems, see "Natural History" in Cohn, 1986 pp. 47–72. Cohn deals primarily with North American collectors, but her observations pertain to Mauro's interests as well.

63   Scarabelli, 1843, p. 15.

64   Belvedere di Saragozza #307, now via Palestro #46 (Guidicini, 1868–73, vol. 1, p. 134); Zanotti, 1925, p. 389, n. 73. Mauro continued to regret the loss of his garden ("Lettere," 16 February 1821).

65   Keates, 1994, p. 180.

66   De Tocqueville, 1969, p. 468.

67   Burrows and Wallace, 1999, p. 337.

68   Greenleaf, 1850, p. 333. William Penn was convinced that Quakers and other Protestant sects not tolerated in Europe deserved religious liberty and easy land terms in the New World, and he gained this in his Province of Pennsylvania for which he obtained a land grant in 1681 from Charles II.

69   Edward Hicks, *Memoirs*, quoted in Weekley, 1999, p. 30.

70   See Voyage, p. 83 and p. 136 n. 75.

71   *New York Spectator*, 26 October 1816.

72   Koke, 1982, p. 208. Vanderlyn was later able to install his Ariadne in the Rotunda in City Hall Park which had been built for the express purpose of exhibiting his panorama of Versailles. The painting was engraved by Asher B. Durand (Stauffer, 1907, vol. 2, p. 116). It is described as "a nude figure lying on the ground asleep. There is a seashore and a boat on the right." The print was copyrighted in London in 1835 as *Ariadne Asleep on the Island of Naxos*.

73   Mauro kept the watercolor all his life and willed it to the executors of his *testamento*, of whom Luigi Sedazzi (a painter and friend in Bologna) was one. It has survived the vicissitudes of time and, still in pristine condition, is now in a Roman private collection.

74   The story of the conflicting interests of the business community who ran the Academy and the Society of Artists, as well as the obstacles that confounded the formation of a teaching facility in Philadelphia is well told by Nygren, 1971.

75   Following the established European academic tradition, life drawing was taught primarily at night. The hours of daylight were reserved for painting, as candle light compromised color judgments.

76   Thackara, following the practice of the Royal Academy, served not only as Keeper of collections but art teacher as well.

77   Nygren, 1971, p. 229.

78   Quoted in Nygren, 1971, p. 224.

79   It was not only the culture-starved New World that prized such copies. At some point between 1811 and his departure in

1816, Mauro made a watercolor copy after Francesco Albani's *Rape of Persephone* and *Dance of Love* for his friend Count Ferdinando Marescalchi, who paid him 30,000 francs for his efforts and praised the results.

80 Cohn, 1986, p. 210.

81 For a discussion of the attribution of this drawing, see Biagi-Maino, 1995, p. 36 and p. 46, n. 69. Mauro derived the likeness, though not the fleas, from the frontispiece portrait of the noted zoologist published in the *Epistolae ad Societam Regiam Anglicam*, London, 1719.

82 The portrait, derived from Palagi's self-portrait in the Uffizi, reflects the mutual affection between the two. When Pelagi learned of Mauro's return from America, he wrote exhultantly to his brother Giuseppe: "Mauro Gandolfi is reborn! The news that he's in Florence is now certain" (letter, 14 December 1816, quoted in Longhi, 1905).

83 Sewell, 1976, pp. 142–3. Benjamin West had made a profit of £14,000 from the engraved reproduction of his *Death of General Wolfe*.

84 Trumbull, 1841, pp. 361, 363–4.

85 Trumbull, 1841, p. 366.

86 The composition of the *Declaration* was designed as early as November 1786, but the completion of the portraits took longer (Sizer, 1953, p. 147, nn. 270 and 272).

87 Letter to Andrew Robertson, 28 June 1816 (D. 94, pp. 792–4).

88 Trumbull, 1841, p. 417.

89 Trumbull, 1841, p. 360.

90 Cowdrey, 1953, p. 150. "The reputation of Durand as an engraver in pure line was established by his large plate of the *Declaration of Independence* after John Trumbull . . . His portrait work has never been surpassed in excellence by an American engraver" (Stauffer, 1907, vol 1, p. 72). An unfinished proof of the *Declaration* in etching only is in The New York Historical Society.

91 The letters are part of the Raccolta Pallotti in the Biblioteca Comunale del' Archiginnasio di Bologna. The collection also includes a draft of Mauro's last will and testament (*testamento*), dated 15 July 1831.

92 "Lettere," 15 November 1821.

93 "Lettere," 10 September 1819.

94 "Lettere," 26 July 1821.

95 Another is in a private collection in Rome.

96 See Cazort, 1987, nn. 26–7.

97 "Lettere," 21 November 1819.

98 "Lettere," 12 January 1821; "Lettere," 28 November 1821.

99 "Lettere," 5 October 1820.

100 "If only you knew the tenor of Protasio's words to me" ("Lettere," 8 November 1821).

101 "Lettere," 27 October 1821.

102 "Lettere," 25 November 1821.

103 "Today it seems better for me to return home, to adjust myself to reality" ("Lettere," 15 December 1822).

104 Guidicini, 1868–73, vol. 4, p. 58, n. 1.

105 *Testamento* (Raccolta Pallotti, Biblioteca Comunale di Bologna).

106 D. Gandolfi, 1862, pp. 8–9.

107 According to Democrito's memoirs written when he was sixty-seven, these words were spoken by his father who had just returned from the Assembly convened in Modena by Napoleon, to which he had been nominated by the Senate of Bologna "per tratarre affari importantissimi della Patria" (to negotiate the very important business of the nation) (D. Gandolfi, 1862, p. 7).

108 D. Gandolfi, 1862, pp. 21–2.

109   She was still living with Mauro in Milan in 1821, and often sent her greetings in the letters to Sedazzi. She had a son, Giulio Nilo Wandolf, mentioned in Mauro's letters as "Giulietto." According to Gualandi's notes to the "Viaggio," Giulio was seventeen in 1834, thus born in 1817. The dates suggest that he may have been Mauro's natural son. In his *testamento* Mauro specifies that Giulio inherit his black ink portraits of Gaetano and of Mauro himself as a young man along with two mappa mundi and a celestial sphere.

110   "Lettere," 30 May 1832.

111   He founded the Italian language department at Columbia University and wrote a delightful memoir of his adventures in the New World. See da Ponte, 1921.

112   Several examples support this assumption, such as James Philip Puglia, a fascinating writer on democracy and the rights of man, who arrived in Philadelphia in 1790 and who left a clear testimony that his accent branded him a "stranger" and non-citizen (Simmons, 1977). In his chapter "Merchants and Entrepreneurs," Richard Juliani suggests that food manufacturers and vendors did better than those who aspired to a higher cultural level, citing Joseph Marble, a wealthy grocer who died in 1821. One John Palma (or di Palma), a mid-eighteenth-century violinist, and John Gualdo, a composer, both failed miserably to succeed in Philadelphia in the years before mass emigration (Juliani, 1997, pp. 5–9).

113   Scarabelli, 1843, p. 6.

114   Scarabelli, 1843, p. 6.

Voyage

1   The manuscript forms part of the Collezioni d'arte e di storia of the Cassa di Risparmio in Bologna (Fondazione Carisbo, Fondo Ambrosini 4507.CIII.op.52). It has a dedicatory overleaf in Gualandi's hand that says, "To my friend Luciano Scarabelli of Piacenza. Michelangelo Gualandi of Bologna, 1834. Text returned to him on 6 July 1866." A second overleaf in Scarabelli's hand (though not reproduced in his 1842 publication) says, "Note from the publisher to the Public. We print the description of the interesting journey to the United States undertaken by a celebrated Italian artist, a text that was offered to me some time ago by a friend, who said enough in his annotation and in his letter as to persuade me to print it just as it is, leaving ample space to the reader who wishes to comment on it in his own way." And Gualandi again, "See how the wish of my friend Scarabelli was indeed put into practice. It may however be necessary to fill in those few gaps which remain, correct the missing words, and the obvious mistakes, etc." Finally there is a letter from Gualandi to Scarabelli: "My Dearest Friend, For a long time now I have been pondering what token of friendship I might venture to offer you, when chance led me to come across an interesting text, deserving (in my opinion) to be dedicated to a friend. This is a journey to the United States that was undertaken between February and October of 1816 by the eminent artist Mauro Gandolfi, engraver and painter, who described it six years later in epistolary form addressing it to a friend in Milan, where he had retired. I shall send it to you, diligently transcribed by me from the original, adding a few little things here and there to ease the way to you in case you intend to publish it. When you come to speak of our Author, and of his contemporaries and fellow artists, you will

find plenty of interesting things to say about their eccentric mode of life, their idiosyncrasies and the air of geniality that characterized those who cultivated the Fine Arts. I have put in parentheses the Italian version of the Author's English words. I have corrected, as far as a beginner is able to do, those English words which were totally wrong, and I have restricted myself to some additional notes, which you may wish to expand as you see fit. The titles of the paragraphs were originally in the margins. I would suppress them and leave only the successive numbers which I have added. You will find the Table of Contents, which is placed after the Introductory Note, useful. To conclude, I wish to express with great pleasure my friendship to you. Michelangelo Gualandi, Bologna, 30 July 1834."

2   The Porte de Peyrou is an imposing arched gateway to the city of Montpellier built in 1692–3.

3   The fear of immigrants had begun earlier, largely in response to the flood of French immigrants, both Royalists and Jacobins, and the refugees from the Irish Rebellion of 1798. The Alien, Sedition, and Naturalization Acts were passed in 1798. The last of these extended the waiting period for citizenship from five to fourteen years.

4   The Supercargo was the officer on a merchant ship whose duty it was to manage the passengers' concerns during the voyage.

5   Apparently the ship passed the northern edge of the Sargasso Sea, a relatively stable sea-within-a-sea held in place by the main circulating currents of the North Atlantic and extending roughly between 25 and 32 degrees Latitude. The Sea is largely composed of a seaweed known as Sargasso, or Gulf weed, which serves as shelter for a unique variety of marine flora and fauna.

6   An unidentifiable botanical term: "Fucus" is a kind of seaweed, or orchella weed; "Bucinalis" would refer to a curved, trumpet-like shape.

7   The ship had been blown off course in a northerly direction. Mauro's note that they were between 42 and 43 degrees latitude accords with the southern edge of the Grand Banks. The sounding would have confirmed this, as the sea depth decreases abruptly there to between 100 and 200 meters.

8   Mauro transliterated this phonetically as "Olijbott".

9   Mauro wrote this in English as, "Earth, earth Gentleman!"

10 One reason for this miscellany was the fact that a few early Dutch houses survived the great fire of 1776 then new structures were built next to them in the eighteenth century.

11 The customs officials at the Port of New York had been, since 1789, officers of the federal government, while those who examined goods being imported were municipal officials. This might explain why Mauro had to shuttle between offices to clear his effects. Wall Street was a major thoroughfare in the earliest part of south Manhattan to be developed.

12 Mauro was referring to his wooden lay figure with moveable parts which artists used to establish poses.

13 Mauro uses English for the childrens' exclamations: "the black, the black of wood."

14 At this point in his narrative, Mauro begins to move between the present and the past tense, sometimes describing the

United States as if it were still 1816, sometimes updating his facts. We have simply adopted his use of tenses.

15   Mauro's citation of the lower latitudinal boundary of the United States as being 31 degrees at the time of his trip was based on the fact that Florida was in 1816 still officially Spanish property, having been ceded to them by England in 1783 as part of the territorial settlement that followed the Revolutionary War. In 1819 Spain ceded all lands east of the Mississippi, including Florida, to the United States in return for the cancellation of $5 million in debt, establishing the territorial boundary as 26 degrees latitude "nowadays." Mauro is less accurate on his description of the northern boundary of the United States as being 49 degrees which would have included, among other things, Montreal. From the conclusion of the War of 1812, Lower Canada's allegiance was to Britain, not the United States.

16   Mauro calculates the birth of the Republic from the date of the end of the Revolutionary War (12 March 1783) and not, as is now fondly supposed by the citizens, from the Declaration of Independence on 4 July 1776.

17   The British burned Washington in August 1814, including the White House and the major governmental buildings. At the time of Mauro's visit the reconstruction had not been completed.

18   Madison completed his second four-year term in March 1817. The election of Monroe was held in November 1820. At this point, Mauro was writing post-facto.

19   Mauro is referring to Daniel D. Tompkins (1774–1825), Governor of New York State from 1807 to 1817.

20   The New York City Directory confirms Mr. Stephen Perpignan's address as being at 26 William Street (Longworth, 1815–16). *Perpignan and Co.*, merchants, were at 139 Water Street.

21   A more modest traveller to New York recorded that for board and lodging in 1817 he paid $4.00, equivalent to 10 shillings, per week (Palmer, 1818, p. 6).

22   I could find no mention of a Chevalier restaurant on Chambers Street, though one Mary Chevalier is listed in the New York City Directory (Longworth, 1815–16) as having a boarding house at 98 William Street. As Mauro lived at 26 William Street, it is not unlikely there would have been some three-way connection between Francophones here.

23   French restaurants became popular in New York in the late 1790s as part of the "gallomania" pervading the city in the wake of the French revolution (Burrows and Wallace, 1999, pp. 322–33).

24   "The houses are generally good, frequently elegant, but it requires American eyes to discover that Broadway competes with the finest streets of London or Paris" (Stokes and Haskell, 1926, vol. 5, p. 1586, quoting from Lieutenant Francis Hall, 1818). "Towards the end of autumn, during the beautiful winter months and in the early spring, the world of elegance parades on Broadway. It is fashionable to be seen out of doors between two and three in the afternoon. The women's clothes are colorful and in good taste. French modes are followed" (Klinckowström, [1824] 1952, p. 117).

25   The New York City Directory mentions a C. D. Vecchio who had a looking-glass and print store at 138 Broadway (Longworth, 1815–16). Broadway, by the time of Mauro's visit, was paved as far north as Canal Street, above which the numbering began in the 400s. After the cessation of hostili-

ties with the British in 1783, Broadway was the focus of efforts on the part of the municipal authorities to upgrade major thoroughfares that were the centers of social and economic importance, along with Wall Street. Broadway was the single most fashionable street in the city.

26 This would have been his *Saint Cecilia Seated at the Organ*, after a painting by his father, Gaetano (see fig. 17). The *Saint Cecilia* after Raphael's famous painting in Bologna was not done until 1834, his last engraving. He seems to be suggesting that this is well above his usual asking price for an engraving.

27 *The Happy Dream* had been titled *Il sogno lieto* by Mauro (see fig. 18).

28 Partition Street, renamed Fulton Street in November 1816, ran west from Broadway.

29 Thomas Gimbrede (1781–1832) came to New York in 1802 as a miniature painter, but by 1810 had become a full-time engraver, doing mainly portraits in the stipple manner for John Low and William Durrell. Trained in France, as was Mauro, his engraving technique was one of the best to be seen in New York at the period. Mauro gives his address correctly as 120 Bowery, with a studio at 201 Bowery (Longworth, 1815–16). The Bowery at this point was paved from the present Broome Street up to what is now 23 Street, thus serving as a major north–south thoroughfare (Burrows and Wallace, 1999, p. 364). Gimbrede also worked in Philadelphia for the illustrated periodicals *Portfolio* and *Analectic*, and may have introduced Mauro to the *Analectic* publisher, Moses Thomas. In 1819 Gimbrede was appointed drawing master at the Military Academy at West Point.

30 John Trumbull (1756–1843) ranks as the major early American painter of his-

torical scenes at the time and a visit from him would certainly have been an honor. He worked as topographical draughtsman during the Revolutionary War then moved to London to study with Benjamin West. After a series of diplomatic posts in Europe, he established a studio in New York in 1804, in 1805 was elected president of the new New York Academy of Fine Arts, and in 1808 became vice president of the American Academy of Fine Arts which had been founded in New York in 1802. This latter organization then foundered and was revived in 1816 newly located at 24 Park Place – at this point Trumbull, thanks to his celebrity, social prominence, and intimacy with major political figures, was elected president (Cowdrey, 1953, p. 16). In this year the artists, who felt slighted by the pomp of the Academy, rebelled and formed the New York Academy of the Arts of Design which consisted of artists and no connoisseurs. Neither organization seems to have recognized Mauro.

31 John Pintard (1759–1844) was a major New York speculator and manipulator of the stock market and president of the New York Bank of Savings (Burrows and Wallace, 1999, p. 309). For a full biography see Cowdrey, 1953 (pp. 628–9). He graduated from the College of New Jersey (Princeton) in 1776, joined his foster father's mercantile business, and later began his own business in trade with China and East India. He lost his fortune in the crash of 1792, but recouped it through insurance business. Primarily interested in history, he helped found the New York Historical Society in 1804 and was its recording secretary from 1805 to 1819. Active also in the renewal of the Academy in 1816, he served as its secretary

from 1815 to 1816 (Longworth, 1815–16, p. 96). John Trumbull painted portraits of him and his wife. He died in New York at age 85.

32   Probably John R. Murray who in 1815–16 was the vice president of the Academy as well as the assistant secretary of the Manumission Society. He lent a *Mary Magdalene* print to an Academy exhibition in 1817. The artist's name is not listed, and it may have been one of Mauro's prints that he had brought with him.

33   Probably Dr. Samuel Latham Mitchill (1764–1831), active as a nationalist and pioneer in sanitary reforms and education. Mauro was inaccurate as to his profession: he was in 1817 still editor of the first medical journal in the United States, the *Medical Repository*, which he had founded, and was the first professor of chemistry, not botany, in the United States. (K. Jackson, 1995, p. 765). Dr. Mitchill had an early interest in lithography and was the recipient of the first lithographic stone to cross the Atlantic (Shadwell, 1986, pp. 17–18).

34   Arthur J. Stansbury (1781–1865). Clergyman and illustrator of *The Grammar of Botany* of 1822, "the first book whose artist and printer are known, illustrated by lithography in America" (Shadwell, 1986, pp. 17–18). Two of his lithographs, one a botanical study of cherries and one a copy after Jacques Callot's "Beggars" of c.1622, are in the New York Historical Society, the latter bearing an inscription, "These first Specimens of American Lithography are respectfully presented to Dr. Mitchill by his Friend A. J. Stansbury."

35   Archibald Robertson was an artist, designer, and etcher who came to the United States from England in 1791 or 1792. From 1792 to 1821 he was a teacher of drawing and watercolor in New York, and in 1793 with his brother Alexander he opened the Columbian Academy of Painting at 89 William Street. He designed for engravers and early lithographers, and drew for engraved views. He also did portrait engravings, including one of Washington.

36   John Vanderlyn who studied at Robertson's Academy in Philadelphia and in 1793, funded by Aaron Burr, went to Paris to study further. He was a member of the American Academy at 24 Park Place, founded in 1816, from 1817 to 1826. A list of his contributions to the Academy's exhibition in 1817 included a *St Cecilia* after Raphael and the *Sortie from Gibralter* after Trumbull (Stauffer, 1907, vol. 2, p. 116). His famed *Ariadne* was engraved by Asher B. Durand, though not copyrighted until 1832 in London. For his biography, see Cowdrey, 1953, p. 363.

37   Michael A. Paff, at 254 Bowery (Longworth, 1815–16), was a merchant of fine art objects (Upton and Howat et al., 2000, p. 22). "Paff's Gallery of Paintings is in Wall Street. The collection consists of nearly three hundred original paintings and about two thousand etchings and engravings" (Blunt, 1818, entry for October 1817). Paff was known equally "for the zeal and taste he has evidenced . . . with the laudable view of improving public taste" and for having "bought, sold, exchanged and jobbed pictures and when required repaired, vanished and repainted them" (Cowdrey, 1955, p. 24).

38   William Satchwell Leney (1769–1831) was trained in stipple engraving in London, a technique he applied to portraits and religious subjects in New York. His extant account book is useful for current prices

charged. For instance, impressions of an octavo engraved portraits went for prices ranging from $100 to $150 in 1812. He engraved the first notes for the Bank of Montreal and a now scarce series of large plates of views in and around Montreal.

39 "Collins and Company," booksellers, stationers, and publishers at 189 Pearl Street consisted of the brothers Isaac and Thomas Collins, one of whom visited Mauro. For the bible they published in 1817 Leney engraved a plate showing "Moses in the Bulrushes," but there was no mention of Mauro.

40 Dr. Archibald Bruce, M.D., was a distinguished physician and minerologist. He is listed in the New York City Directories for the years 1815–16 and 1816–17.

41 In Philadelphia in 1817, "There are many prostitutes but they are easily distinguished from the rest of society, seldom prowling the streets late at night and never, I believe, addressing people as they pass. Prostitution is less here than in a place the same size in England and absolute proverty infinitely so" (Palmer, 1818, p. 289).

42 "I have good reason for stating that in this country the food is gobbled" (Klinckoström, [1824] 1952, p. 26).

43 Meals on the road from New York to Philadelphia in 1817 were described elsewhere as "Our supper consisted of a mixture of good things in all parts of the Union: beef steaks, fried bacon, peach preserves, short cakes, bread and butter, coffee and tea for which, with a bed and two glasses of toddy, we paid 75 cents each" (Palmer, 1818, p. 13).

44 Azam's situation was far from unique. The demand for clothing and shoes in the ever expanding population encouraged the proliferation of the "artisan-entrepreneur," whose profits depended on exploiting cheap labor, usually that of new immigrants (Burrows and Wallace, 1999, p. 346).

45 Mauro was referring to the ancient Greek city of Corinth, known for its elegance and sophistication, as the symbol of every traveller's desire but beyond poor Mr. Azam's capabilities.

46 "Oysters! They sell from 12 cents to $2.00 per hundred. There are many oyster stands in the city, where black men are ready with some of the finest oysters which they open and serve out raw for 1 and 3 cents apiece with some salt and pepper" (Wood, [1808] 1931, p. 44).

47 And for a different interpretation, "About the break of day, after the morning gun is heard from Governor's Island, and so on through the forenoon, the ears of the citizens are grated with this unearthly sound, from figures as unpleasant to the sight, clothed in rags and covered with soot, a necessary and suffering class of human beings indeed, much to be pitied . . . spending their childhood thus which ought to be spent in getting learning" (Wood, [1808] 1931, p. 48).

48 The New York State Legislature's "Gradual Manumission Act" of 1799 had freed those children born to slaves after 4 July of that year and planned for gradual manumission, though it did not allow current slaves to be freed. Slaves born before 4 July 1799 were not finally freed until 1827. Although by 1810 New York had the largest community of free negroes in North America, slaveholding was still common there, with domestic service to the rich being a standard occupation of blacks. Few were trained in the trades as the supply of low wage, white immigrant

labor was ever replenished. "From and after the first day of May, 1810, no person held as a slave shall be imported, introduced, or brought into this state on any pretence whatever by a person or persons coming permanently to reside within the same, and that any person residing within this state for the space of nine months shall be considered as having a permanent residence therein . . . and if any person so held as a slave shall be so imported, introduced, or brought into this state contrary to the true intent and meaning of this act, he or she shall be and is hereby declared free . . . Some malfeasors have manumitted their slaves to N.Y. to work for certain inhabitants long enough to work off their value, this declared illegal, bond void, slave free. Anybody importing slaves must make an oath or affirmation before a judge, mayor, recorder, alderman, or Justice of the Peace to this effect. Failure to do so frees the slave. Selling of a slave is a public offence, fee $250. Importation of slaves for selling is illegal. If a slave strikes a white person, on oath of same to Justice of the Peace the slave goes to jail, is tried, and punished as in petit larceny. In all other cases, slaves have right to trial by jury" (Blunt, 1818, Appendix XIX, "Slaves and Servants", pp. 299–305).

49   Mauro's opinion was not unique. "The colored race, most of whom are free, are the most shameless and insolent people of the masses here and are not considered equals in Society. Hence they put no limit to their impertinences, so very irritating because they lack all culture. The majority of blacks are lazy, belligerent and discourteous." (Klinckoström, [1824] 1952, p. 81).

50   According to the exchange rates listed in the City Directory (Longworth,

1815–16), one pound sterling equalled $4.44. Another contemporary gives the Golden Eagle as $10.00, the Silver as $5.00. Exchange rates were apparently fluid at the time.

51   Brutus, as a member of the group who conspired to slay Julius Caesar, was a symbolic hero during the French Revolution. He personified the idealistic republican who places duty to country above ties of family and friendship.

52   The illuminations or moving transparencies of these parades were huge paintings on cloth of patriotic subjects that were backlit with candles after dark (Burrows and Wallace, 1999, pp. 297–8). The description of the Fourth of July parade in Philadelphia in 1808 describes such "transparencies" of Washington and Jefferson (Brigham, 1995, p. 32).

53   The *New York Evening Post* and several other newspapers advertised events celebrating the Fourth of July: "Joseph Delacroix' Vauxhall Gardens: The gardens will be decorated in all parts by a number of elegant paintings executed by the first artists, and which will be lighted up in the evening. There will be lamps and transparent vases . . ." (the *New York Evening Post*, 3 July 1816). The New York daily, *Commercial Advertiser* for July 3 promised: "A grand transparent painting will be exhibited in allusion to the day. On the right hand is Liberty, represented by an allegorical female figure, clad in robes of yellow, beneath her feet a globe; in one hand she holds the Standard of the United States, and is supposed to be in the act of planting it . . . On the left are three Boys, one of whom is holding and pointing to a book, in the open leaf of which is seen written: Declaration of Independence,

July 4, 1776. In the centre, the American Eagle, hovering over and covering a globe. Tomorrow evening will be presented (for the first time in America) the drama of THE BATTLE OF NEW ORLEANS or the Glorious Eighth of January. Between the Play and Farce, Mr. Van Voorhis will dance a NAVAL HORNPIPE. Mr. Pritchard will sing 'We have met the enemy and they are ours' and 'Tea Table Chat, or what will Mrs. Grundy say?' by Mr. Baldwin. The evening's entertainments to conclude with the Grand Serious Pantomine of "Three Finger'd Jack." The *New York Gazette and General Advertiser* prints the additional promise of "Grand Fire-Works at Vauxhall Gardens . . . to be celebrated in the first style of Splendor and Elegance." Baron Klinckowström described at length the celebrations of the Fourth of July in 1819 as featuring a ship's model, music, and a parade to City Hall. On Thanksgiving, the Order of Masons read the Declaration of Independence, spokesmen from the stone-cutting industry read Washington's Farewell Address, and there was a big dinner (Klinckoström, [1824] 1952, p. 116).

54 For Inauguration Day 1788 the Confederated Congress designated New York as the temporary seat of government. In 1800 the New York City Common Council planned for a new City Hall to be built on the old Common, a spacious lot with a variety of shade trees. The architectural competition was won by Joseph-Francois Mangin and John McComb. Benjamin Henry Latrobe's splendid design, the drawings for which are today with the Library of Congress, was rejected probably on the basis of cost. Mangin's building, essentially a more modest version of Latrobe's, was begun in 1803 and com-

pleted in 1811. As it was then on the northern edge of the city, the back of the building was faced with brownstone, instead of the marble that faced the façade, as a cost saving measure. It exists today much as it was originally built. "The City Hall is the most prominent and important structure in the United States, perhaps of its size in the world. This chaste and beautiful edifice stands near the upper end of the park and is seen to advantage from every quarter" (Palmer, 1818, p. 307).

55 On receiving an invitation to meet President Monroe, Baron Klinckowström protested that he did not have the proper formal dress. His contact "laughed and assured me that one need not be so particular in this country . . . There was no Honor-Guard and the President wears a plain brown coat" (Klinckowström, [1824] 1952, p. 26).

56 It is instructive to compare Mauro's enthusiastic description of 4 July 1816 with that of John Pintard in his letter of 5 July to his daughter: "Yesterday the forthieth year of our National Existence was celebrated as usual with the greatest splendor and rejoicing in our city." He goes on to describe in the blandest possible fashion the fact that the weather was clement. He moralizes about the need for good public behavior on such occasions and the virtues of home pleasures. There is no mention of the parade (Pintard, 1940, p. 16).

57 I could find no mention of this practice. If not something of Mauro's invention, it sounds like some version of the English "Lord of Misrule" day.

58 "The Battery, which was intended as a promenade for the recreation of the citizens and was, last summer, tastefully laid out at great public expense, is now become

a place for strolling cows to pasture in and for hogs to root up into a thousand furrows" (*New York Evening Post*, 5 February 1816). A memorandum from the marshal for public peace to the Common Council of 1808 noted that "many persons were in the practice of turning Cows upon the Battery and dusting Carpets and drying clothes thereon, to the great annoyance of the public convenience" (quoted in Deák, 1988, p. 170).

59   Police responsibilities in New York City expanded considerably after the appointment of a vigorous High Constable in 1802. Under his command were sixteen elected constables and seventy-two members of the watch. These monitored public assemblies, interfered forcibly if necessary in disturbances, and made arrests.

60   The Governor at that time was Mauro's friend Tompkins.

61   Vauxhall Gardens, owned and operated by a Mr. Delacroix, was a park with gravelled walks, trees, an equestrian statue of Washington, and shrubs that ran along Fourth Avenue near Astor Place, between Broadway and the Bowery at 8th Street (Stokes and Haskell, 1926, vol. 5).

62   Penal reforms in New York in 1796 had reduced capital offenses to three: treason, murder, and theft from a church (Burrows and Wallace, 1999, p. 366). "Treason, murder, and arson of an inhabited dwelling house were formerly the only offenses punished with death in this state. April 15, 1817 it was broadened to include burning prisons or killing policemen" (Palmer, 1818, p. 322).

63   The *Commercial Advertiser* gave considerable attention during the month of August 1816 to the execution of Richard Smith, a twenty-year-old sailor who killed a Captain Cook in a fit of anger. The newspaper played up in tabloid fashion a "singular document" entitled the "Dying Confession of Richard Smith." Published in several newspapers, it purported to be a letter from the unfortunate Smith to his wife, Ann, in which he bemoaned his lot, but confessed to his regrettable crime of passion. The *Advertiser* claimed, "There cannot exist the smallest doubt of its being the work of some inventive genius and that Smith never saw it, much less dictated it." The paper went on to warn that it has received advance notice of a "core of swindlers and pick-pockets in this city. It is supposed that they are gathering, preparatory to the execution." The Thursday after the execution, which had taken place on Saturday 10 August, a detailed account appeared of Smith's activities and deportment up to his execution, with a lurid description of the crowd's behavior and the unsuccessful attempts to convince Governor Snyder, known to be opposed to capital punishment, to pardon him. In Philadelphia a Quaker lady recorded her reactions: "August 10. Today poor Smith was executed . . . I do not think I ever so realized to myself the situation of a condemned criminal, as I said in this instance and most sincerely do wish the Governor had extended his clemency to the unhappy sufferer . . . He has covered my mind with gloom, and I hope he has met with mercy from his Creator" (Logan, 1816–17, p. 21).

64   Mauro was referring to Bellevue, a complex of buildings at 26th Street and First Avenue overlooking the East River. Originally the Almshouse, it was converted into the City Penitentiary in 1816. Like all penal institutions of the period

it attempted to distinguish between the "deserving" and the "undeserving" poor, or between those reduced to institutional living through dire poverty or through crime. The line was continually blurred as such institutions became overcrowded almost as soon as they were built. "The alms or poorhouse stands in the suburbs, on East River. It is a large stone structure, three stories high, in the center four, with a handsome cupola. It was opened to the reception of paupers in 1816 . . . The number of inmates in August 1817, was 1,487" (Palmer, 1818, p. 311).

65   The mobility restrictions that Mauro describes applied only to debts of a fairly minor order, and these "gaol limits" were gradually extended to include areas where most of the working men lived, since they made up the majority of the indebted. Debtors were also imprisoned from 1814 until 1838 in The Bridewell, a large brick building with pediments and four chimneys which had been built in 1775–6 as a prison on a site west of the City Hall. In 1817 a law was passed ending all jail sentences for debtors who owed less than $25.00.

66   Mauro seems to be trying to adjust his description to the understanding of his untravelled Bolognese friend. His allusion to the old Roman Road and its ruined gate, and the Lazzaretto, would refer to the outermost circle of city walls still intact in Mauro's day.

67   For an assessment of New York's place as the primary "hub of speculation," see Burrows and Wallace, 1999, pp. 336–7. The drive to "get rich" was particularly evident during the period of Mauro's visit. One incentive, following the victory over the British in 1783, was the exodus of the Loyalist sympathizers, the aristocracy of pre-Revolutionary New York, who often sold lock, stock, and barrell to emigrate, and whose properties were purchased by eager patriots.

68   "Fire! Fire! Fire! This is a dismal and alarming call indeed in the night . . . The rattling of the engines, the burning and falling houses, the destruction of goods and sometimes lives . . . yet the consternation and loss . . . are not sufficient to prevent some abandoned wretches from stealing" (Wood, [1808] 1931, p. 3).

69   In 1801, in a belated reaction to the great fire of 1776, the state legislature granted the municipal government power to enforce building codes, which included a requirement that all new buildings be built of brick or stone and have slate roofs. This proved ineffective, and on 11 April 1815 a new law stated that "The Legislature requires that all houses between the Battery and a line drawn from the Hudson River through Jay Street to the East River at Montgomery Street be constructed of brick and stone for the more effectual prevention of fires" ("Laws of New York," 1815, in Stokes and Haskell, 1926, vol. 5, p. 1581).

70   A stagecoach advertisement in the *Commercial Advertiser* of 7 May 1816 gave the fare from New York to Philadelphia as $5.50, and from New York to Albany as $7.00. New York to Philadelphia by boat cost $5.00 in 1817 (Palmer, 1818, p. 6).

71   Stagecoaches left for Boston, Albany, and Philadelphia from Fraunces Tavern.

72   Here one encounters another of Mauro's impenetrable terms: "Psiticus dei Tronchili ardea."

73   Pigs were apparently ubiquitous: "In the city of New York on a moderate calcula-

tion several thousand pigs are suffered to roam about the streets, to the disgrace of the corporation and danger of passengers. A law was passed prohibiting their being at large after January 1818, but before it went into operation it was repealed" (Palmer, 1818, p. 6).

74   The bridge at Trenton was a single-span wooden bridge built around 1812. Mauro's "pertica," or "perch," is approximately equal to 27.5 yards, though it varied locally.

75   Mauro may have been unaware, though the lady perhaps was not, that on 1 July 1816 a law was enacted that prevented swimming and bathing "at improper times and places and for other purposes" (*Minutes of the Common Council of the City of New York 1784–1831*, vol. 8, 1814–17). Even earlier, "The Corporation says no bathing south of the State Prison, in the North River at Delancey Street, or in the East River between 6 a.m. and 8 p.m." (Wood, [1808] 1931, p. 50).

76   The "famous traveller" refers to Napoleon. After agreeing to lead the French expedition to Egypt in 1796, he is reported to have said to his soldiers, "Songez que, du haut de ces pyramides, trente siècles nous contemplent" (Stendhal, 1961, Chapter x).

77   By 1806 New York had surpassed Philadelphia in size and in the value of its export as well as its import trade, but Philadelphia still held the cultural edge. The beautification program undertaken after the Revolution frequently elicited comments from admiring visitors and Benjamin Latrobe, the major architect of the period, called it "The Athens of America." William Russell Birch prefaced his series of etched views of the city in 1800 with a similar encomium: "It has in this short time been raised as it were by magic power to the eminence of an opulent city."

78   Mauro's designation of the English Quaker as "the famous Dutch philosopher" indicates his casual attitude towards both philosophy and history. He may also have misunderstood, as have many subsequently, the phrase "Pennsylvania Deutsch."

79   "The private buildings are generally three stories high, they are built with a fine red brick and ornamented in white marble" (Paxton, 1811, p. 11). It was fashionable in both Philadelphia and New York from the 1780s on to paint the mortar of the brick houses in a contrasting color. "Wooden houses are prohibited being built within the most populous parts of the city, under a penalty of $500.00" (Palmer, 1818, p. 290).

80   Mauro would have seen Benjamin Latrobe's great Doric Bank of Pennsylvania and the majestic Bank of the United States, its pedimented Corinthian façade faced with marble. Like the City Hall in New York, cost-consciousness decreed that the other three sides were built of brick.

81   It is impossible to verify this charming custom. However, a stroll through the older residential areas of such well-preserved towns in southern Pennsylvania as Lancaster show the houses separated by a narrow walkway or "tradesmen access," barred by a simple wooden gate closed by a latch, parallel to the façades of the houses, though toolsheds have now replaced the outhouses at the end of the walkway. Now, as then, they often maintain flower gardens between the front door and the street.

82   Mauro would have been especially struck by the configuration of the streets in contrast to his own "patria" Bologna, where

except for the radials the streets were all curved with porticos.

83   The current Reading Market, as well as markets in such towns as Lancaster, follows this layout. Philadelphia's wide streets justifiably excited Mauro's admiration. He claimed that Market Street was the widest in the city, but another source gives its width as 100 feet (Palmer, 1818, p. 253). High Street was 100 feet wide and Broad Street 113 feet (Paxton, 1811, p. 11).

84   Mauro was referring to the First Chestnut Street Theatre, built in 1807, and subsequently burnt and rebuilt twice (Jackson, 1931, vol. 2, p. 422).

85   Moses Thomas is listed in the City Directory of Philadelphia as "bookseller, 52 Chesnut Street," an address substantiated by Fielding in Stauffer, 1917, vol. 3, p. 256. He was also a publisher. In 1812 he acquired the "monthly eclectic" magazine the *Select Review* and hired Washington Irving as editor. The name of the periodical was changed in 1813 to the *Analectic Magazine*, and Irving quit in 1814. It published "articles on travel and science . . . The illustrations were usually engravings on copper but some of the earliest magazine experiments in lithography and wood-engraving appeared here" (Mott, 1957, pp. 279–80). It is not known whether or not Mauro contributed any illustrations.

86   Mauro was referring to the State House, now known as Independence Hall, was originally designed by Andrew Hamilton in 1729 and modelled on contemporary English architecture. The building as we know it was the work of Edmund Wooley and his carpenter Ebenezer Tomlinson in 1835. Mauro's description is accurate, except that at no time were the side wings higher than the central block. Gualandi's

transcription, "i due laterali sono piu alti del centro" may be the fault here.

87   Mauro is speaking here about the Peale Museum, founded by Charles Willson Peale (1741–1827) as a picture gallery in 1782. It expanded to become America's first natural history museum in 1786 (Sewell, 1976, p. 117). In New York, Mauro's acquaintance John Pintard had made active efforts to establish, between 1791 and 1795, a museum of American history and natural science, but at the time of Mauro's visit there had been no progress (Burrows and Wallace, 1999, p. 316).

88   Mauro lists four artists: "Chastel, Cuvie, Toin, David." They remain unidentifiable, probably because of either Mauro's or Gualandi's spelling.

89   The museum's most notorious exhibit in Mauro's day was a mastodon fossil skeleton, excavated and installed by Charles Willson Peale himself between 1806 and 1808 (Brigham, 1995, pp. 38–44, fig.9).

90   He is probably referring to the fine anatomical pastels, some by Jan van Rymsdyk, now with the Pennsylvaina Hospital.

91   James Thackara (1767–1848). His name appears in the Philadelphia City Directories as an engraver from 1791 to 1833, and in 1816 was listed as living at 35 Spruce Street (Robinson, 1816). He specialized in line engraved "subject plates" (mainly religious or historical incidents) which adds an ironic twist to Mauro's chastising him on the subject of American artists' ignorance of figure drawing. In 1814 he published "Thackara's Drawing Book for the Amusement and Instruction of Young Ladies and Gentlemen." According to Stauffer (1907, vol. 1, pp. 267–8) he was "for some time after 1826 keeper at the

Philadelphia Academy of Fine Arts," though Mauro speaks of him as "director" in 1816. With his son, William Thackara, he founded the firm of Thackara and Son, a general engraving firm, in 1832.

92   Mauro was being a bit unfair to suggest that puritanism in the arts was restricted to America. He notes in a letter to Luigi Sedazzi (26 July 1821) that he was doing an engraving after Pelagio Palagi, in which "I have added a bit of drapery [to the male figure] to cover that focus of the chief crime of humanity, and the source of its most terrible woe."

93   He may have been referring to Benjamin West's *Penn's Treaty with the Indians* of 1771–2, owned by the Pennsylvania Academy of Fine Arts.

94   C. R. Leslie engraved some line vignettes and title pages for Thomas's *Analectic Magazine* and other Philadelphia publications (Fielding in Stauffer, 1917, vol. 3, p. 256).

95   Gilbert Stuart Newton.

96   Washington Allston's *The Prophet Elijah Raising the Dead Man.*

97   This would have been the firm of Murray, Draper, and Fairman which from 1810 until 1870 was the chief producer in the United States of bank note engravings (Stauffer, 1907, vol. 1, p. 69). It is listed in the City Directories of Philadelphia for 1816 as being situated at 47 Sanson Street (Robinson, 1816). George Murray was listed in the City Directories of Philadelphia as "engraver, 49 and 47 Sanson Street (Robinson, 1816). John Draper was listed from 1801 to 1845 as "engraver". He also engraved for Dobson's edition of Ree's *Encyclopedia*, 1794–1803. Gideon Fairman (1774–1827) began as an engraver of silver plate. In 1818 with Jacob Perkins and Asa

Spencer he went to London to compete for a prize offered for the means of preventing bank note forgeries, evidently a growing problem. Later with Charles Heath he published prints by a "patent hardened steel process" (possibly steel facing). Fairman is listed in the Phildelphia City Directory as having an office near 30 South Seventh, with a dwelling on the southwest corner of Chesnut and Seventh (Robinson, 1816).

98   Mauro referred earlier to Mme Fillette, with whom he boarded (p. 88). One "F. Filette" is listed in the City Directory as having a boarding house at 129 South Second Street (Robinson, 1816).

99   Oddly, Mauro did not comment on the blacks in Philadelphia. A contemporary traveller mentioned that they are "happy, and encouraged by the Friends" (Palmer, 1818, p. 288).

100   "Edward Chaudron, watchmaker and jeweller, 9 South Third Street" (Robinson, 1816). Edward was the son of Simon Chaudron, a French watchmaker and jeweller who had immigrated to Santo Domingo and thence to Philadelphia around 1793 or 1794. The family were also important silversmiths.

101   Mauro's dealing in gems after his return to Italy is shown in many of the letters to his friend Luigi Sedazzi, where he discourses on the rubies and emeralds he is selling.

102   The "old immigrant" Mauro speaks of is probably Simon Chaudron who, with three of his sons including Edward, moved in 1819 to the newly founded town of Demopolis, Alabama. This settlement was termed the "Vine and Olive Colony." Chaudron, as a Francophone from Santo Domingo, would have been another patron of Fillette's. His family later moved

to Mobile, Alabama and continued to work as silversmiths and clockmakers (Sewell et al, 1976, p. 227).

103 Klinckowström writes of the waterworks at Schuylkill in 1818–1820: "Two mighty steam engines of 70 HSP each draw up the water by pumps and it is forced through iron pipes up an 80 foot steep incline near the works. Here the water is caught in a large deep reservoir from which it later is directed down to the city (Klinckowström, [1824] 1952, p. 49). A note to his translation by Franklin D. Scott adds, "Philadelphia had built the first municipal waterworks in America in 1799–1801 with wooden pipes and a reservoir on the site of the old British fort at Fairmount" (p. 49, n. 8).

104 The Fairmount Waterworks, with its steam-powered pump, its terrace, and fountains, was an engineering and architectural feat that elicited panegyrics from the likes of Mark Twain and Frances Trollope throughout the nineteenth century. Mauro is incorrect in asserting that the Fairmount system, designed and constructed by Frederick Graff between 1812 and 1815, was the first example of a steam-powered pump for a public water supply. The Watering Committee, directed by Benjamin Latrobe, had installed steam pumps in Philadelphia's Center Square in 1801. The first of Graff's engines was in operation by 1815, and pumped water from the Schuylkill River to a reservoir with a capacity of three million gallons, since demolished and replaced by the Philadelphia Museum of Art. The cost of fueling the steam pumps was too high, and they were replaced by water-powered pumps in 1822. Mauro states that the pipes for water distribution were of cast iron, with a capacity of three million gallons. Apparently in 1816 replace-

ment of the old bored pine and spruce logs was only at the discussion stage, and not implemented until 1819. The waterworks successfully served the growing city of Philadelphia with water for drinking, cleaning the streets, and firefighting at a time when New York was still subsisting on an inadequate city reservoir with water from local wells pumped by horse power (Gibson, 1988).

105 Such "shot towers" were apparently quite common in that part of the United States. Molten lead was poured through a sieve at the top, the spherical globules landing in a pail of water at the bottom.

106 Mauro was describing the famous "Colossus" bridge over the Schuylkill downstream from the Fairmont dam. It was a single span, covered, wooden arch bridge with a very low rise which was destroyed by fire around 1820. "The handsome Schuylkill bridge, the wooden bridge is built sturdily and the great span of its arch demonstrates the daring of its design" (Klinckowström, [1824] 1952 p. 18).

107 Mauro seems to be referring to "The Hills," a vast acreage on the edge of the city just upstream from the Fairmount Waterworks (Scharf and Westcott, 1884, vol. 3, p. 1826). It had been bought by the financier Robert Morris (1733–1806), who had settled in Philadelphia in 1787, and planted with extensive gardens. Morris fell on hard times, and was in debtors' prison from 1798 to 1801. The property was acquired by Henry Pratt, son of the painter Matthew Pratt, at the sheriff's sale in 1799, at which time Morris built the house named Lemon Hill. Pratt improved the gardens, soon also known as "Pratt's Gardens." He lived at the country house until the middle of the 1830s, so the gar-

dens would have been well maintained at the time of Mauro's visit.

108   The presence of the agave, a semi-tropical plant, indicates that Mr. Morris's famous stone greenhouses were still in working order in 1816.

109   "The antipathy of many of the backwoods men to Indians . . . proceeds, amongst more recent causes, from the dreadful tale they have heard their fathers tell, of Indian cruelty and massacres done by them on the often defenseless first settlers" (Palmer, 1818, p. 101).

110   Colonel Thomas Dongan, the second English governor of New York and himself a Roman Catholic, commented on the variety of religions in 1682: "Here bee not many of the Church of England; few Roman Catholicks; abundance of Quakers, preachers men and women especially; singing Quakers, ranting Quakers, Sabbatarians, Antisabbatarians, some Anabaptists, some Independents, some Jews, in short of all sorts of opinions there are some, and the most part of none at all.' Greenleaf lists the following miscellany of religions as having established churches in New York in 1850: Lutheran (both German and Dutch), Reformed German Lutheran, Calvinist, Moravian (or United Bretheren), Associated Reformed (Presbyterian?), Unitarian, Israeliti, and Friends (Greenleaf, 1850).

111   Mauro is making a jocular reference to equatorial zones where the sun is directly overhead. The peculiar habits of boa constrictors is another of his tall tales of uncertain origin.

112   Robert Fulton, an Irish–American born in Pennsylvania, had developed his invention of the steamboat in Paris. In 1806 he moved to New York and by 1807 his first flat-bottomed boat, 146 feet long and with steam-powered paddle wheels, made its maiden voyage up the Hudson River. The boat was patented in 1809 (Burrows and Wallace, 1999, p. 341). By 1812 six such boats were in service. On 18 April 1815 the Fulton Steamboat Company was incorporated, with the "right to exclusive navigation of the waters of the East River, or Sound, by the means of steam or fire" ("Laws of New York," 1815, in Stokes and Haskell, 1926, vol. 5, p. 1581). On May 21 1816.

113   Catholicism in New York had a complex history. In the early period, organization and maintenance of the churches was prohibited by the Dutch and English Protestants. By 1700 laws were in effect that prevented Catholic priests from entering the colonies on pain of life imprisonment. Intolerance persisted through the first half of the eighteenth century, peaking with the so-called "Negro plot" of 1741 in which Catholics were accused of encouraging slave revolts. In 1784 the anti-priest law was repealed and an Irish Capuchin Charles Whelan established the first permanent Catholic parish in New York. The first Roman Catholic church in the city was a small wooden building on the corner of Barclay and Church Streets, dedicated to St. Peter in November 1786. In 1808 Pius VII established the Diocese of New York. Construction on the imposing St. Patrick's cathedral was begun as early as 1809, and was at first intended to be a structure to measure 120 × 80 feet on the corner of Mott and Prince Streets. By the time it was finished in 1815 it had been extended another 36 feet to reach all the way to Mulberry Street, where it still stands (K. Jackson, 1995, p. 254). On 6 May 1816 the Cathedral was dedicated in the presence of

about 4000 people. "This grand and beautiful church which may justly be considered one of the greatest monuments of our city, and inferior in point of elegance to none in the United States, is built in the Gothic Style, and executed agreeably to the design of Mr. Joseph L. Mangin, the celebrated architect of New York. It is 120 feet long, 80 wide and 75 to 80 high" (*New York Evening Post*, 11 May 1815). This is the church that Mauro described, though I have not been able to identify the "frightful Calvary."

114 1 May 1815: "The Common Council receives and agrees to accept an invitation from the trustees of St Peter's church to attend the dedication of the Cathedral of St. Patrick on Thursday next" (*Minutes of the Common Council 1784–1831*, vol. 8, p. 195, in Stokes and Haskell, 1926, vol. 5, p. 1582).

Unfortunately Mauro could not have attended the opening of the Cathedral as he only arrived in New York a year later, although this does not affect the veracity of his story about the music which follows.

115 The double program of a tragedy and a comedy was the usual nightly billing at the Park, New York's only theater at the time. Newspapers from the summer of 1816 mention *Jane Shore* as a tragedy. An undated playbill of Booth's Theater announced *Jane Shore!*, apparently a drama of the English monarchy that entailed lords, ladies, ruffians, beggars, and a notable snow scene. I have not found *Killing No Murder*, Mauro's version of the comedy's title (Odell, 1927, pp. 455 ff).

116 "The public is respectfully informed that the Park Theater will be opened on Monday, the 3rd of September. Preparations have been in the making during the last season and the recess, for various and extensive alterations . . . likely to increase the comfort or the convenience of the audience. An entirely new plan of decoration has been completed for the interior of the house, and the effect produced is more striking and brilliant than any heretofore seen in America" (*New York Evening Post*, 26 August 1816). "A correspondent says in regard to the newly decorated Park Theater, 'It literally presents that gaiety and elegance of a drawing room, without any allow whatsoever of gaudiness. The fronts of the boxes are most tastefully decorated with classical ornaments relieved in gold upon a white ground, and the unity of this preserved throughout . . . the boxes a delicate peach blossom tint. The columns, ostensibly appearing to support the different tiers, give the effect of gold which not only contributes to the richness of the whole, but admirably impress, from their massive appearance, the purpose of support to which they are appropriated'." (*New York Evening Post*, 4 September 1816). This theater, built between 1795 and 1798 and redecorated in 1816, burned down in 1820. A new theater was built but also burned down in 1848 and was never replaced.

117 Mrs. Barnes was popular in the New York season of 1816 which began in September. In 1815 she had been described as "petite, well proportioned, her features are good and when elevated by dignity, by impassioned sentiment, are impressive," and "the best Juliet on the American stage" (*New York Evening Post*, 18 April 1815) Her portrait as "Isabella" was engraved by Asher B. Durand after J. Neagle in 1825 (Odell, 1927, p. 453). She often performed with her husband, Mr. Barnes, who featured in one of the Fourth of July extravaganzas that year, *Barney, leave the girls alone*! (*New York Evening Post*, 4 July 1816).

118 On 13 June 1815 the Common Council

granted the use of the Alms House, in the rear of City Hall, to various learned and cultural societies for no less than seven and no more than twenty-one years. The third floor was for the Academy of Arts and the notice asking artists to submit "specimens of their talent" to the first exhibition was posted on 30 September 1816. The exhibition opened to the public with great success on 25 October 1816 (Cowdrey, 1953, pp. 15–19). Its stated purpose was to form "a united collection of statuary and painting, which in point of excellence is unrivelled [*sic*] in this country, etc." The second floor was for the American Museum (of Natural Science). A contemporary account describes its contents: "There is a small museum in New York, the best part of which is a collection of birds, well preserved; and the worst, a set of wax work figures, among whom are Saul in a Frenchman's embroidered coat, the Witch of Endor in the costume of a House-maid, and Samuel in a robe de chambre and cotton night cap" (Stokes and Haskell, 1926, vol. 5, p. 1586, quoting Lieutenant. Francis Hall, 5 March 1816). This museum, while still located at 21 Chatham Street, advertised itself in the City Directory of 1815–1816 (Longworth, 1815–16) as follows: "An Extensive and splendid collection of some of the largest and smallest of nature, and of the works of Art from every quarter of the globe." It enumerates scientific specimens and wax models. Finally, there was to be on the first floor the New York Society Library, the New York Historical Society, and the New York Literary and Philosophical Society. One room was for the display of mechanical inventions, another for a cabinet of minerology, another for a lecture hall, and one for an "apparatus chamber." The basement was

to house a chemical laboratory (*Minutes of the Common Council*, vol. 8, pp. 232–6 in Stokes and Haskell, 1926, vol. 5, p. 1583) which may explain the disastrous fire of 19 January 1854. In May of 1816 the paupers had been relocated to a new facility at Bellevue which had been remodelled to accommodate them. At this point occupancy was in the name of the newly founded New York Institution of Learned and Scientific Establishments (Burrows and Wallace, 1999, pp. 467–8).

119   According to a glowing account in the *New York Spectator* of 26 October 1816, a ticket to the opening cost only twenty-five cents a head (quoted in Cowdrey, 1953, p. 18). Mauro's status as an outsider is shown by the fact his works were not included (though whether this was his choice is not known) and he was apparently not invited to the private viewing on 24 October 1816. Curiously, a list of the works shown in the 1816 exhibition included a mention of some prints with no indication as to artist. Mauro's friend Dr. Bruce lent a *Madonna* after Guido Reni, and another friend J. R. Murray lent a *Mary Magdalene* and *Arcadian Shepherds Discovering a Tomb*. These could well be prints by Mauro, but if so it is strange that he did not mention them. In the exhibition of 1817, Dr. Bruce lent a *Nativity* and a *Sleeping Boy*, again unattributed in the list and possibly by Mauro.

120   Mauro was probably referring to Louis Antoine Collas (1775–1856). A painter of portraits and miniatures, Collas was born in France but was in New York in 1816, by which time he had anglicized his name to Lewis Collers (Groce and Wallace, 1957, p. 140). He was active as a portraitist in St Petersburg from 1808 to 1811, and between 1811 and 1822 in New Orleans (*The*

Encyclopedia of New Orleans Artists 1718–1918, 1987). He may also have been the "Colles" in "Messers. Vanderlyn, Colles, and Milbert have the honor to announce that they have established in this city an Academy of Drawing and Painting" (Stokes and Haskell, 1926, vol. 5, p. 1586, quoting from the *New York Evening Post*, 1 May 1816).

121   See p. 26 and fig. 16.

122   This turned out to be one of Gimbrede's most successful portrait prints, a stipple etching with engraved accents. There are at least two almost identical versions, the smaller one (Stauffer, 1907, vol. 2, p. 1067) being somewhat stiff, the larger more accomplished. The latter bears the inscription, "James Monroe President of the United States engraved by T. Gimbrede from an original painting by I. Van Der Lyn." Vanderlyn's original study for his painting, which is what Mauro apparently saw, is not to be found.

123   Alexander Anderson (Stauffer, 1907, vol. 1, pp. 8–9). Born in New York City in 1775 and thus eleven years Mauro's junior, Anderson graduated as a Doctor of Medicine from Columbia in 1796. After losing his wife and infant son as well as his brother, mother, and father to the Yellow Fever epidemic of 1798, he abandoned his medical practice to devote himself to wood engraving, inspired by the pioneer in this field, Thomas Bewick, and became the "father of wood engraving in the United States" by engraving Bewick's *General History of Quadrupeds* for its American edition of 1804. He died in Jersey City in 1870. Washington Irving described Anderson as "handsome, artless, and gentle as a woman," which accords with his generosity towards Mauro. The bible Mauro mentions may well have been one

with Anderson's own illustrations.

124   Siderography was one of the innumerable techniques of reproductive printmaking developed in the early nineteenth century. Specifically, it was a method of engraving on steel credited to Jacob Perkins around 1820. It was often used to produce banknotes (Harris, 1970, p. 193).

125   See Henry Clay's address to Congress in 1818 in which he expresses a similar sentiment.

126   The young man can be identified as William Main (1796–1876), who would thus have been twenty years old at the time (Groce and Wallace, 1957).

127   *Limulus polyphemus*. Mauro was justifiably fascinated by the horseshoe crab, a species of marine creature found along the eastern North American coast. Structurally it is intermediate between crustaceans and arachnids. Fossil specimens dating from 500 million years ago have been found. Since they live in the sand near the shore, it is likely that Mauro found a dead one floating rather than a live one swimming. His fantastic tale about how it eats an oyster is probably a fable fed to him by the sailors.

128   A web-footed bird with a forked tail that hatches its eggs under its wings fits no known zoological description. Mauro may have been pulling his reader's leg.

129   This is not so far-fetched as it appears. Seasickness on a tossing vessel is exacerbated by watching an immoveable horizon or land line.

130   We have transcribed Mauro's botanical and zoological spellings literally.

131   The reference to the equinox here remains inexplicable.

132   It appears that Teresa was expected to revert here to her role as Mauro's domestic servant.

Bibliography

Apell, Alois. *Handbuch für Kupferstichsammler oder Lexicon der vorzüglichsten Stecher des XIXten Jahrhunderts*, Leipzig, 1880.

L'Avvenire d'Italia (newspaper).

Bagni, Prisco. *I Gandolfi: Affreschi, dipinti, bozzetti, disegni*, Bologna, 1992.

Bentini, Jadranka, et al. *Arte e pietá*, Bologna, 1980.

Biagi-Maino, Donatella. *Gaetano Gandolfi*, Turin, 1995.

Bianchi, Lidia. *I Gandolfi*, Rome, 1936.

Blunt, Edmund M. *Stranger's guide to the city of New York to which is prefixed an historical sketch, general description and extent of the city*, New York, 1818.

Bourne, George M. Untitled (illustrations of New York, published series of 19 plates, 1830–31, drawn by C. W. Burton with various engravers).

Brigham, David R. *Public Culture in the Early Republic: Peale's Museum and its Audience*, Washington and London, 1995.

Brown, H. Glenn, and Maude O. *A Directory of the Book Arts: Book Trade in Philadelphia to 1820*, New York Public Library, New York, 1950.

Burrows, Edwin G., and Mike Wallace. *Gotham: A History of New York City to 1898*, Oxford and New York, 1999.

Cavazza, Giulio. "Bologna dall'età napoleonica al primo Novecento (1796–1918)," in *Storia di Bologna*, 1978, pp. 285–391.

Cazort, Mimi. "I Gandolfi: i disegni" in *L'arte del Settecento emiliano: La pittura, l'Accademia Clementina*, exh. cat., Bologna, 1979.

——. "Il disegni di Ubaldo, Gaetano e Mauro Gandolfi nelle collezioni della Fondazione Giorgio Cini," in *I Gandolfi, Ubaldo, Gaetano, Mauro*, exh. cat., nos. 1–54, Vicenza, 1987.

——. "Gaetano Gandolfi's Children's Portraits," in *European Drawings from Six Centuries: Festschrift to Erik Fischer*, Copenhagen, 1992, pp. 87–98, figs. 1–6.

——. "The Art of Embellishment: Some Drawings and Paintings for a Festive Carriage," in *The Record of the Art Museum, Princeton University*, Princeton, 1993a, vol. 52, no. 2, pp. 22–38.

——. "An Introduction to the Gandolfi," in *Bella Pittura: The Art of the Gandolfi*, and cat. nos. 1–43, exh. cat., National Gallery of Canada, Ottawa, and Little Rock, Arkansas Arts Center, Bologna, 1993b.

——. "Some Early Drawings by Mauro Gandolfi," *Master Drawings*, vol. 33, 1995, no. 2, pp. 144–51, figs. 1–7.

Cohn, Marjorie B. *Francis Calley Gray and Art Collecting for America*, Cambridge, 1986.

Cowdrey, Mary Bartlett. *American Academy of Fine Arts and American Art-Union Exhibition Record: 1816–1852*, with a history of the American Academy by Theodore Sizer, The New York Historical Society, New York, 1953.

Da Ponte, Lorenzo. *Memoirs of Lorenzo da Ponte*, trans. and ed. Elizabeth Abbott and Arnold Livingston, Philadelphia, 1921 (originally published as *Mémoires de Lorenzo da Ponte prêtre vénitien collaborateur de Mozart. Traduite de l'italien per M.C.D. de la Chavanne*, Paris, 1860).

De Tocqueville, Alexis. *Democracy in America*, ed. J. P. Mayer and trans. George Lawrence, New

York, 1969 (originally published as *La Démocratie en Amérique*, Paris, 1835).

Deák, Gloria Gilda. *Picturing America 1497–1899: Prints, Maps and Drawings Bearing on the New World Discoveries*, Princeton, 1988.

Emiliani, Andrea. *La Pinacoteca Nazionale di Bologna*, Bologna, 1967.

The Encyclopedia of New Orleans Artists 1718–1918, New Orleans, 1987.

Fanti, Mario. "Bologna nell'etá moderna," in *Storia di Bologna*, Bologna, 1978, pp. 199–282.

Farneti, F. "I maestri dell'Accademia Clementina," in *Atti e memorie dell'Accademia Clementina*, vol. 23, Bologna, 1988.

Fielding, Mantle. *Dictionary of American Painters, Sculptors and Engravers with an addendum containing corrections on the original entries compiled by James F. Cart*, New York, 1965.

Filby, P. William, and Mary K. Meyer, eds. *Passenger and Immigration Lists Index Being a Guide to Published Lists of Arrivals in the United States and Canada*, 2 vols., Detroit, 1981.

Gandolfi, Democrito. *Di alcuni fatti politici antecedendti alla guerra liberatrice del 1859, i quali influirono sulla vita dello scultore Democrito Gandolfi, figlio del celebre incisore bolognese*, Bologna, 1862.

Gandolfi, Mauro. "Lettere," Biblioteca Comunale dell'Archiginnasio di Bologna, Autografi raccolti da Ciprano Pallotti e da lui legatati al Municipio di Bologna, vol. XIV, 6, nos. 815–81.

Gibson, Jane Mork. "The Fairmount Waterworks," *Bulletin of the Philadelphia Museum of Art*, vol. 84, 1988, nos. 36–361.

Goldoni, Luca, Aldo Ferrari, and Gianni Leoni. *I Giorni di Bologna: Kaput*, Bologna, 1980.

Gottesman, Rita Susswein. *The Arts and Crafts in New York*, The New York Historical Society, New York, 1965.

Greenleaf, Jonathan. *The Churches of All Denominations in the City of New York from the First Settlement*, New York, 1850.

Groce, George C., and David H. Wallace. *The New York Historical Society Dictionary of Artists in America 1564–1861*, New Haven and London, 1957.

Guidicini, Giuseppe. *Graticola di Bologna*, Bologna, 1844.

———. *Cose notabili della città di Bologna ossia Storia Cronologica de' suoi stabili sacri, pubblici, e privati*, 4 vols., Bologna, 1868–73.

———. *Diario bolognese dal anno 1796 al 1818 con un cenno cronologico dei governi di Bologna dalla sua fondazione in poi . . .*, Bologna, 1886–7 (published by his son Ferdinando).

[?Gualandi, Michelangelo]. "Patria necrologica," in *Gazzetta privilegiata di Bologna*, 14 January 1834 (Mauro Gandolfi's obituary).

Hall, Lieutenant Francis. *Travels in Canada and the United States in 1816 and 1817*, London, 1818.

Harris, Elizabeth. "Jacob Perkins, William Congreve, and Counterfeit Printing in 1820," in *Prints In and Of America to 1850*, ed. John D. Morris, (Winterthur Conference Report), Charlottesville, 1970.

Holdcamper, Forrest R., comp. *List of American Flag Merchant Vessells that Received Certificates of Enrollment or Registry at the Port of New York 1789–1867*, intr. Kenneth R. Hall, 2 vols., Washington, 1968.

Isham, Samuel. *The History of American Painting*, New York, 1905.

Jackson, Joseph. *Encyclopedia of Philadelphia*, 4 vols., Harrisburg, 1931.

Jackson, Kenneth T., ed. *The Encyclopedia of New York City*, New Haven and London, 1995.

Juliani, Richard N. *Building Little Italy: Philadelphia's Italians before Mass Migration*, Philadelphia, 1997.

Keates, Jonathan. *Stendhal*, New York, 1994.

Klinckowström, Freiherr von. *Baron Klinckowström's America 1818–1820*, trans. and ed. Franklin D. Scott, Evanston, 1952 (originally published as *Bref om de Förente Staterne, författade under en Resa till America aren 1818, 1819 och 1820*, Stockholm, 1824).

Koke, Richard J. *A Catalogue of the Collection, including Historical, Narrative, and Marine Art*, 3: *American Landscape and Genre Paintings in the New York Historical Society*, New York, 1982.

Kouwenhoven, John A. *The Columbia Historical Portrait of New York: An Essay in Graphic History*, foreword by Grayson L. Kirk, New York, 1953.

Levitine, George. "French Eighteenth-Century Printmaking in Search of Cultural Assertion" in *Regency to Empire: French Printmaking 1715–1814*, Minneapolis, 1984, pp. 10–21.

Lewis, Benjamin M. *A Guide to Engravings in American Magazines 1741–1810*, New York Public Library, New York, 1959.

Logan, Deborah Norris. "Diaries," vol. 2, May 1816–June 1817, MS, Pennsylvania Historical Society, Philadelphia.

Longhi, Alessandro. "Mauro Gandolfi e suo viaggio in America," in *Il resto del carlino*, 23, 24 February, 1905; 28, 29, 30 December, 1906; 1, 3, 5, 7, 8, 9, 10, 11, 13, 14, 15 January, 1907.

Longworth, David. *Longworth's American Almanac: New York Register and City Directory for the Fortieth Year of American Independence*, New York, 1815–16.

McKee, George D. *The Art of Drawing Art*, Binghampton, N.Y., 1993.

McKusker, John. "How Much is That in Real Money?" in *Proceedings of the American Antiquarian Society*, place, 1993.

Milbert, Jacques Gérard. *Itinéraire pittoresque du fleuve Hudson et des parties latérales de l'Amérique du Nord*, Paris, 1828–9.

Minutes of the Common Council of the City of New York 1784–1831, vol. 8, 1814–17, The New York Historical Society.

Montulé, Édouard de. *Voyage en Amérique, en Italie, en Sicile et en Égypte pendant les années 1816, 1817 et 1819*, Paris, 1821.

Moscow, Henry. *The Street Book: An Encyclopedia of Manhattan Street Names and Their Origins*, New York, c.1978.

Mott, Frank Luther. *A History of American Magazines 1741–1850*, Cambridge, Mass., 1957.

The New York Historical Society, *Catalogue of American Portraits*, New Haven, 1974, 2 vols.

Nygren, Edward J. "The First Fine Art Schools at the Pennsylvania Accademy of the Fine Arts," *The Pennsylvania Magazine*, vol. 95, 1971, no. 2, pp. 221–38.

Odell, George Clinton Densmore. *Annals of the New York Stage*, 2: *1798–1821*, New York, 1927.

Oriole, Emilio. "Mauro Gandolfi e il tricolore," *Il resto del carlino*, 29 July 1903.

Pairpoint, Alfred J. *Uncle Sam and his Country, or Sketches of America in 1854, 1855, 1856*, London, 1857.

Palmer, John. *Journal of travels in the United States of North America and in Lower Canada performed in the year 1817 containing particulars relating to the price of land and provisions, remarks on the country and people, interesting anecdotes . . .*, London, 1818.

Paxton, John Adems. *The Sranger's Guide: An Alphabetical List. All the Wards, Streets, Roads, Lanes, Alleys, Avenues, Courts, Wharves, ShipYards, Public Buildings, etc. in the City and Suburbs of Philadelphia*, Philadelphia, 1811.

Perkins, James H. *Annals of the West embracing a concise account of the principal events which have occurred in the western states and territories from the discovery of the Mississippi valley to the year eighteen hundred and forty five . . .*, 2nd ed., rev. and enlarged J. M. Peck, St. Louis, 1850.

Pintard, John. *Letters from John Pintard to his daughter Eliza Noel Pintard Davidson*, 4 vols., The New York Historical Society, New York, 1940, 1: *1816–1820*.

Poch, Robert, "John Trumbull: Painter of the American Revolution," *American History Illustrated*, vol. 18, November 1983, no. 7, pp. 18–23.

Pomeroy, Jane. *Alexander Anderson's life and engravings with a checklist of publications drawn from his diary*, Worcester, Mass., 1990.

Riccomini, Eugenio. *Il Settecento a Ferrara*, Cento, 1971.

Robinson, James. *The Philadelphia Directory for 1816 Containing the Names, Trades and Residence of the Inhabitants of the City*, Phildelphia, 1816.

Roli, Renato. *Pittura bolognese 1650–1800: Dal Cignani ai Gandolfi*, Bologna, 1977.

Rosenberg, Pierre, and Odile Sebastiani. "Trois berlines peintes par Mauro Gandolfi," *Antologia di Belle Arti*, vol. 1, 1977, no. 3, pp. 225–44.

Roversi, Giancarlo, and Valerio Montanari. *Le grande biblioteche dell'Emilia-Romagna e del Montefeltro*, Milan, 1991.

Scarabelli, Luciano. "Viaggio agli Stati Uniti di Mauro Gandolfi" *Il Vaglio. Giornale critico, scientifico, artistico, letterario*, vol. 3, 1842, no. 23 (6 June), no. 25 (20 June), no. 26 (27 June), no. 27 (4 July), no. 45 (7 November), no. 46 (14 November), no. 50 (12 December), no. 51 (19 December), no. 52 (26 December).

———. "Mauro Gandolfi," in *Opuscoli artistici, morali, scientifici e letterarii*, Piacenza, 1843, pp. 3–19.

Scarabello, Giovanni. *Processo a Da Ponte*, Venice, 1989.

Scharf, J. Thomas, and Thompson Westcott. *History of Philadelphia: 1609–1884*, 3 vols., Philadelphia, 1884.

Schiavo, Giovanni E. *Four Centuries of Italian American History*, New York, 1958.

Sewell, Darrel, et al. *Philadelphia: Three Centuries of American Art*, exh. cat., Philadelphia Museum of Art, Philadelphia, 1976.

Shadwell, Wendy. *"Prized Prints": Rare American Prints before 1860 in the Collection of The New York Historical Society*, imprint 11 (Spring 1986), pp. 1–27.

Simmons, Merle E. *Santiago F. Puglia: An Early Philadelphia Propagandist for Spanish American Independence*, Chapel Hill, 1977.

Sizer, Theodore. *The Works of Colonel John Trumbell, Artist of the American Revolution* (revised edition), New York, 1953.

Stauffer, David McNeely. *American Engravers upon Copper and Steel*, New York, Philadelphia, and Worcester, Mass., 3 vols., 1907, 1917 and 1921: vol. 1: *Biographical Sketches Illustrated*, New York, 1907; vol. 2: *Check List of the Works of the Earlier Engravers*, New York, 1907; vol. 3: *American Engravers: A Supplement to David McNeely Stauffer's American Engravers*, by Mantle Fielding, Philadelphia, 1917; supplement: *An Artist's Index to Stauffer's American Engravers*, by Thomas Hovey, Worcester, Mass., 1921.

Stendhal, Henry Beyle. *La Vie de Napoleon*, 1816–1836, Lausanne, 1961, chapter 10.

Stokes, I. N. Phelps. *American Historical Prints: Early Views of American Cities, etc. From the Phelps Stokes and other Collections*, New York Public Library, New York, 1933.

———, and Daniel C. Hashell. *The Iconography of Manhattan Island, 1498–1909*, New York, 1915–28, vol. 5, chapter 5, part A: "As the War of 1812; 1812–1815", New York, 1926; part B: "Period of Invention, Prosperity and Progress 1815–1841," and vol. 6, Index, New York, 1926.

"La Storia del Tricolore Italiano", in *Archivio emiliano del risorgimento italiano*, Modena, 1907.

Svin'in, Pavel Petrovitch. *Picturesque United States of America, 1811, 1812, 1813*, New York, 1930.

Teitelman, S. Robert. *Birch's Views of Philadelphia: A Reduced Facsimile of* The City of Philadelphia *as it appeared in the year 1800*, Philadelphia, 2000.

Tonini, Luigi. *Guida del forestiere nella città di Rimini . . .* , Rimini, 1864.

Trumbull, John. *Autobiography, Reminiscences and Letters, 1756–1841*, New York, London and New Haven, 1841, chapter 18: "1808–1816."

Upton, Dell, and John K. Howat, et al. *Art and the Empire City: New York, 1825–1861*, exh. cat., The Metropolitan Museum of Art, New York, 2000.

Vail, R. W. G. *Knickerbocker Birthday: A Sesqui-Centennial History of The New York Historical Society 1804–1954*, The New York Historical Society, New York, 1954.

Volpe, Carlo. "I Gandolfi," in *L'Arte del Settecento emiliano: La pittura, L'Accademia Clementina*, exh. cat., Bologna, 1979.

Weekley, Carolyn J. *The Kingdoms of Edward Hicks*, New York, 1999.

Wintermute, Alan, with Colin B. Bailey, William Olander, and Carol S. Eliel. *French Art During the Revolution*, exh. cat., Colnaghi, London, 1989.

Wood, Samuel. *The Cries of New York*, New York, 1931 (originally published in 1808).

Wright, Frances. *Views of society and manners in America in a series of letters from that country to a friend in England during the years 1818, 1819 and 1820*, New York, 1821.

Zanotti, Augusto. "Brevi cenni della vita di Mauro Gandolfi bolognese. Pittore, disegnatore ed incisore a taglio reale. Prefazione, note e vignette di Augusto Zanotti," *Comune di Bologna*, vol. 11, 1925, no. 2, February, pp. 73–81; no. 3, March, pp. 145–153; no. 6, June, pp. 388–93.

Zanotti, Mauro. *Origine e storia della bandiera d'Italia*, Bondeno, 1941.

Zecchi, Giovanni. *Collezione dei monumenti sepulcrali del Cimiterio di Bologna pubblicata da Giovanni Zecchi stampatore e negoziante di stampe*, 4 vols., Bologna, 1825–7.

———. *Descrizione della Certosa di Bologna ora Cimitero comunale*, Bologna, 1828.

Zucchini, Guido. "Communicazione dell'Accademico Guido Zucchini su quadri e disegni inediti di Gaetano Gandolfi", in *Atti e memorie dell'Accademia Clementina*, Bologna, 1953, pp. 49–60.

Illustrations

1 Gaetano Gandolfi, *Portrait of Mauro at Age Four*, 1768, oil on canvas. Private collection, Bologna. Photograph: Antonio Guerra, Bologna.

2 Mauro Gandolfi, *The Cistern of the Palazzo Pubblico, Bologna, with Vagabonds at Rest*, date unknown, pen, brown ink, and wash over black chalk. Dusseldorf, Kunstmuseum. Photograph: Landesbildstelle Rheinland.

3 Mauro Gandolfi, *The Farewell*, c.1788, oil on canvas. Gabinetto dei Disegni e delle Stampe della Pinacoteca Nazionale di Bologna, Dono Ghedini Foto. Photograph: Matteuzzi-Mattioli.

4 Mauro Gandolfi, *Carriage of the Tanari Family, with "Calypso Receiving Telemachus and Mentor"*, c.1789, oil on panel, gilded wood. Musée Nationale du Chateau, Compiègne (Oise). Photograph: Hutin, © By Spadem Paris.

5 Mauro Gandolfi, *Allegory of Astronomy*, c.1789, pen, brown ink, and blue, rose, yellow, and brown washes over black chalk. The Metropolitan Museum of Art, Rogers Fund, 1961, 61.130.2. Photograph: The Metropolitan Museum of Art, New York.

6 Mauro Gandolfi, *Seated Male Nude*, 1792, black chalk heightened with white. Accademia di Belle Arti, Bologna. Photograph: Accademia di Belle Arti, Bologna.

7 Mauro Gandolfi, *Clementina*, date unknown, etching. Private collection.

8 Mauro Gandolfi, *Self-Portrait as a Young Man*, c.1782, oil on canvas. Collection Francesco Molinari Pradelli, Marano di Castennaso (Bologna). Photograph: Antonio Guerra, Bologna.

9 Mauro Gandolfi, *Self-Portrait at Age Thirty*, 1794, oil on canvas. Pinacoteca Nazionale di Bologna. Galleria Cavour, Bologna.

10 Mauro Gandolfi, *St. Dominic Burning the Books*, 1790, oil on canvas. Ferrara, Church of St. Dominic. Photograph: Soprintendenza Beni Artistici e Storici, Bologna.

11 Mauro Gandolfi, *St. Francis and the Pilgrims*, c.1790, oil on canvas. Private collection. Photograph: Fotofast, Bologna.

12 Mauro Gandolfi, *The Healing Vision of St. Pellegrino Laziosi*, date unknown, pen, brown ink, and brown wash. Graphische Sammlung Albertina, Vienna. Photograph: Fonds Albertina, Vienna.

13 Mauro Gandolfi, *Repubblica Cisalpina*, c.1797, etching. Stone–Hill, inc., New York. Photograph: Charles Duncan, New York.

14 Mauro Gandolfi (after Cristofano Allori), *Judith with the Head of Holophernes*, 1817–24, engraving and etching. Philadelphia Museum of Art: The Muriel and Philip Berman Gift, acquired from the John S. Phillips Bequest of 1876 to the Pennsylvania Academy of Fine Arts, with funds contributed by Muriel and Philip

Berman, gifts (by exchange) of Lisa Norris Elkins, Bryant W. Langston, Samuel S. White 3rd, and Vera White, with additional funds contributed by John Howard McFadden, Jr., Thomas Skelton Harrison, and the Philip H. and A. S. W. Rosenbach Foundation. Photograph: Lynn Rosenthal, 2002.

15   Mauro Gandolfi, *Sheet of Eight Fantastic Heads*, date unknown, pen and brown ink. Formerly London art market. Photograph: Prudence Cumings, London.

16   Asher B. Durand (after John Vanderlyn), *Ariadne Asleep on Naxos*, 1832, engraving. Photograph: © Collection of The New York Historical Society, New York.

17   Mauro Gandolfi (after Gaetano Gandolfi), *St. Cecilia Seated at the Organ*, before 1816, engraving. Philadelphia Museum of Art: The Muriel and Philip Berman Gift, acquired from the John S. Phillips Bequest of 1876 to the Pennsylvania Academy of Fine Arts, with funds contributed by Muriel and Philip Berman, gifts (by exchange) of Lisa Norris Elkins, Bryant W. Langston, Samuel S. White 3rd, and Vera White, with additional funds contributed by John Howard McFadden, Jr., Thomas Skelton Harrison, and the Philip H. and A. S. W. Rosenbach Foundation. Photograph: Lynn Rosenthal, 2002.

18   Mauro Gandolfi, *The Happy Dream*, 1811, brush and watercolor on vellum. Private collection, Rome.

19   Detail of fig. 23.

20   Thomas Gimbrede and Mauro Gandolfi (after Wheeler), *Major General Andrew Jackson of the United States Army*, 1816, engraving with etching. Photograph: © Collection of The New York Historical Society, New York.

21   Mauro Gandolfi, *Portrait of Anton van Leeuwenhoek*, date unknown, pen, black and brown ink, brown and gray wash. The Metropolitan Museum of Art, New York. Mrs. Carl L. Selden Gift, in memory of Carl. L. Selden, 1987.

22   Mauro Gandolfi, *Portrait of Pelagio Palagi*, c.1820, oil on canvas. Private collection, Bologna.

23   Mauro Gandolfi, *Love Sleeping*, c.1820, engraving and etching. Philadelphia Museum of Art: The Muriel and Philip Berman Gift, acquired from the John S. Phillips Bequest of 1876 to the Pennsylvania Academy of Fine Arts, with funds contributed by Muriel and Philip Berman, gifts (by exchange) of Lisa Norris Elkins, Bryant W. Langston, Samuel S. White 3rd, and Vera White, with additional funds contributed by John Howard McFadden, Jr., Thomas Skelton Harrison, and the Philip H. and A. S. W. Rosenbach Foundation. Photograph: Lynn Rosenthal, 2002.

24   Anne-Marguérite-Henriette Rouillé de Marigny, Baroness Hyde de Neuville, *The Family of Baron Hyde de Neuville in Their Ship's Cabin*, June 1816, watercolor. Photograph: © Collection of The New York Historical Society, New York.

25   Baron Axel Leonhard Klinckowström, *Harbor and Docks of New York from Brooklyn on Long Island*, 1824, aquatint. Photograph: © Collection of The New York Historical Society, New York.

26   John Hill (after William Guy Wall), *Manhattan from Brooklyn Heights, New Jersey in the Distance*, 1823, aquatint. Photograph: © Collection of The New York Historical Society, New York.

27   John Joseph Holland, *Broad Street looking*

toward Old Federal Hall, with Dutch Gabled Houses, 1797, watercolor. The Phelps Stokes Collection, Miriam and Ira D. Wallach Division of Art, Prints and Photographs, The New York Public Library, Astor, Lenox and Tilden Foundations.

28 George Hayward, *Houses on William Street*, 1800, lithograph. Photograph: © Collection of The New York Historical Society, New York.

29 William James Bennett, *Broadway from the Bowling Green*, c.1826, aquatint. Photograph: Collection of The New York Historical Society, New York.

30 Asher B. Durand (after John Trumbull), *The Signing of the Declaration of Independence*, 1824, engraving and etching. Photograph: © Collection of The New York Historical Society, New York.

31 Detail of fig. 30.

32 Nicolino Calyo, *The Oyster Stand*, c.1840, watercolor. Photograph: © Collection of The New York Historical Society, New York.

33 Nicolino Calyo, *The Chimney Sweep at Rest*, c.1840, watercolor. Gift of Mrs. Francis P. Garvan in memory of Francis P. Garvan. Photograph: © Museum of the City of New York.

34 Baron Axel Leonhard Klinckowström, *Broadway Street and the City Hall*, 1819, aquatint. Photograph: © Collection of The New York Historical Society, New York.

35 William Guy Wall, *New York City Hall*, 1826, aquatint. The Phelps Stokes Collection, Miriam and Ira D. Wallach Division of Art, Prints and Photographs, The New York Public Library, Astor, Lenox and Tilden Foundations.

36 Anonymous, *Alms House Hospital, Bellevue as City Penitentiary*, c.1820, lithograph. Photograph: © Collection of The New York Historical Society, New York.

37 Anne-Marguérite-Henriette Rouillé de Marigny, Baroness Hyde de Neuville, *Bridewell, and Charity School, Broadway*, 1808, watercolor. The Phelps Stokes Collection, Miriam and Ira D. Wallach Division of Art, Prints and Photographs, The New York Public Library, Astor, Lenox and Tilden Foundations.

38 Anne-Marguérite-Henriette Rouillé de Marigny, Baroness Hyde de Neuville, *Corner of Greenwich and Dey Streets*, 1810, watercolor. The Phelps Stokes Collection, Miriam and Ira D. Wallach Division of Art, Prints and Photographs, The New York Public Library, Astor, Lenox and Tilden Foundations.

39 Nicolino Calyo, *The Head Foreman*, c.1840, watercolor. Gift of Mrs. Francis P. Garvan in memory of Francis P. Garvan. Photograph: © Museum of the City of New York.

40 Detail of fig. 37.

41 William Birch, *View in Third Street from Spruce Street, Philadelphia*, 1799, etching. The Library Company of Philadelphia.

42 William Birch, *The Bank of the United States, Philadelphia (later Girard's Bank)*, 1798, etching. The Library Company of Philadelphia.

43 William Birch, *High Street from Ninth Street, Philadelphia*, 1799, etching. The Library Company of Philadelphia.

44 William Birch, *The High Street Country Market*, 1799, etching. The Library Company of Philadelphia.

45   William Birch, *The Back of the Statehouse with Indians*, 1799, etching. The Library Company of Philadelphia.

46   B. Tanner after John James Barralet, *The Pennsylvania Academy of Fine Arts*, 1809, lithograph. The Library Company of Philadelphia.

47   Nicolino Calyo, *A Quakeress*, c.1840, watercolor. Gift of Mrs. Francis P. Garvan in memory of Francis P. Garvan. Photograph: © Museum of the City of New York.

48   R. Campbell (after Thomas Birch), *View of the Dam and Water Works at Fair Mount, Philadelphia*, 1824, engraving. The Library Company of Philadelphia.

49   Anonymous, *The Promenade at the Fairmount Waterworks*, c.1836, lithograph. The Library Company of Philadelphia.

50   Baron Axel Leonhard Klinckowström, *Upper Ferry Bridge, Schuylkill River*, c.1819, aquatint. Photograph: © Collection of The New York Historical Society, New York.

51   A. Lawson after John James Barralet, *North View of the Schuylkill Bridge*, date unknown, etching. The Library Company of Philadelphia.

52   Detail of fig. 45.

53   Anne-Marguérite-Henriette Rouillé de Marigny, Baroness Hyde de Neuville, *Tonavente, Peter of Bufalo, an Iriquois of the Niagara Region*, c.1810, watercolor. Photograph: © Collection of The New York Historical Society, New York.

54   William Kneass (after William Strickland), *Masonic Hall, Chestnut Street, Philadelphia*, 1813, engraving. The Library Company of Philadelphia.

55   John Hill (after Samuel Jones and John Lewis Krimmel), *The Burning of the Masonic Hall*, 1819, aquatint. Photograph: © Collection of The New York Historical Society, New York.

56   Benjamin Tanner (after John James Barralet), *Launch of the Steam Frigate Fulton the First at New York, 29 October 1814*, date unknown, aquatint. Photograph: © Collection of The New York Historical Society, New York.

57   Nicolino Calyo, *The Bowery Boys*, c.1840, watercolor. Photograph: © Collection of The New York Historical Society, New York.

58   Anonymous, *Broadsheet, "Jane Shore"*, date unknown, letterpress. Photograph: © Collection of The New York Historical Society, New York.

59   John Searle, *Interior of the Park Theatre, New York*, 1822, watercolor. Photograph: © Collection of The New York Historical Society, New York.

Index

Numbers in italic indicate the page on which an illustration appears; information may also be in a caption, which may appear on the page facing the illustration.

Academy of Fine Arts, New York 26, 107, 129n.30
Academy of Fine Arts, Philadelphia 27, 30, 31–2, 89–90, *90*
Accademia Clementina, Bologna 8–9, 11, 19
Accademia di Belle Arti, Bologna 122nn.30, 34
Adorno, Francesco Saverio 5
adultery: avoidance 67–8
Africa 109, 113, 114
agave 96
agriculture *see* farming in America
Albani, Francesco 124–5n.79
Albany, New York 104
Aldrovandi, Count Ulisse 23
Algeria, siege of 114
Allied bombing of Bologna 2, 43, 120n.13
Allison, Mr. (passenger) 109
Allori, Cristofano: *Judith with the Head of Holophernes* *21*
Allston, Washington: *Elijah Resuscitating the Dead Man* 31, 90–91
Alms House, New York 142n.118
Almy, Captain Peter 1, 52, 55, 61
Alps 23, 50–51
altarpieces 14–15
American Academy of Fine Arts 129n.30, 130n.36
American Museum of Natural Science, New York 142n.118
Analectic Magazine 88, 129n.29, 138n.94
ancestor worship in America 100
Anderson, Alexander 108
Angli, Mr. (passenger) 109
animals 80, 93–4, 109–10, 114
Archangeli, Francesco 122n.32
architecture
    of New York 24, 57, *58*, 78, *79*
    of Philadelphia 84–5, 86–7, 88, *89*, 98–9
Armenian Jews 117–18
art in America
    aversion to nudes 26–7, 30, 31, 83, 89–90, 91, 107
    "manikin" confounds customs 59

New York exhibition rooms 107–8
Philadelphia collections 88–90
respect for Italian work 63
teaching of 30–31, 91
    see also printmaking; reproductive engraving
artillery volley off Gibraltar 115
astronomy allegory 6, *8*
atheism 98
Avignon 51
Avvenire d'Italia, L' 2
Azam, Mr. (French shoemaker) 69

Bank of the United States, Philadelphia 85, 136n.80
banknote engravings 37, 131n.38, 138n.97, 143n.123
bankruptcy 77–8
Bardi, Luigi 39
Barnes, Mr. (actor) 141–2n.117
Barnes, Mrs. (actress) 104
Barralet, John James *90*, *95*, *101*
Barras, Paul 20
Battery Park, New York 75
beauty of Americans 66, 67
begging prohibited in America 76–7
Bellevue almshouse and penitentiary, New York 76–7, 77, 134–5n.64, 142n.118
Bennett, William James *62*
Bergins, Consul 109
Bewick, Thomas 143n.122
Beyle, Henri (Stendhal) 23
Bézier 51
Bibiena, Antonio 39
Bible engravings 37, 91, 108
Birch, Thomas *94*
Birch, William Russell
    on Philadelphia 136n.77
    views of Philadelphia *84*, *85*, *86*, *87*, *89*
birds 80, 110, 112–13
black people
    chimney sweeps 25, 70, *71*
    domestic duties 68
    freed slaves 70–71, 131–2n.48
    living conditions in New York 69–70
    in Philadelphia 138n.99
    unreliable character 70–71
Blunt, Edmund M. 130n.37, 132n.48

boa constrictor myth 100–01
Bologna
    Accademia Clementina 8–9, 11, 19
    Allied bombing 2, 43, 120n.13
    Botanical Gardens 33
    cemetery 18, 44
    Cisalpine Republic 19, 121n.22
    Cispadane Republic 16–17, 18–19
    demand for religious art 11, 14–16
    Gonfalionieri 8
    Institute for Science and the Arts 20
    Mauro's houses in 22–3, 43
    Palazzo Bentivoglio 6, 43
    Palazzo Comunale 19–20
Bonaparte, Joseph 90, 120n.12
Bonaparte, Napoleon see Napoleon I
Bordeaux 51–2
    embarkation from 1, 23, 52–3
botanical gardens
    Bologna 33
    Philadelphia 25, 95–6
Bowery, New York 64, 105, 108
Bridewell, New York 78, 81, 135n.65
bridges
    Schuylkill wooden bridge 94–5, 95
    Trenton wooden bridge 82–3
Broadway, New York 61, 62, 73, 78, 81, 128–9n.25
Bruce, Dr. Archibald 67, 142n.119
Brunswick, New Jersey 80, 102
Brutus: Washington as 73
Burr, Aaron 130n.36

Callot, Jacques 130n.34
Calvary painting in New York 102
Calyo, Nicolino: New York scenes 70, 71, 79, 105
Campbell, R. 94
capital punishment in America 76
Caprara, Carlo 6, 17
Carolinas: boa constrictor myth 100–01
carpenter (model of modesty) 67
carriages 6, 8, 9, 33
Cassa di Risparmio, Bologna 2, 119n.4, 126n.1
Castiglione, Luigi 2
Catholicism
    in America 102–3
    decline in religious art in Bologna 11, 14–16
cemeteries
    Bologna 18, 44
    Philadelphia 100
Certosa cemetery, Bologna 18, 44
Chalcographie du Louvre 20
Chalcographie française 20
Chaudron, Edward 92–3

Chaudron, Simon 138n.100, 138–9n.102
Chestnut Street, Philadelphia
    Masonic Hall 98, 99
    theater 88, 137n.84
Chevalier, Mr. (restaurant owner) 61
Chevalier, Mary 128n.22
chickens on board ship 111–12
chimney sweeps in New York 25, 70, 71
churches in America 98, 102–3
Cisalpine Republic 19, 121n.22
Cispadane Republic 16–17, 18–19
City Hall, New York 73–4, 73, 74, 75
City Hall, Philadelphia 88
climate
    of New York 72
    of Philadelphia 88
Cohn, Marjorie B. 32
Collas, Louis Antoine ("Cola") 107
Collins, Mr. (Isaac or Thomas) 66, 108
"Colossus" bridge, Schuylkill 94–5, 95
Columbian Academy of Painting, New York 130n.35
Columbianum art academy, Philadelphia 30
Columbus, Christopher 73
commerce 68–9, 77–8, 92
Commercial Advertiser 132–3n.53, 134n.63, 135n.70
    "confession" of Richard Smith 134n.63
    ships' listing 119n.3
Commission of Veterans' Administration, Bologna 43–4
Congress 60
Constitution: proposed amendments 108
cooking: American disregard for 68
copies of old masters 20, 31–2
    Mauro's skill as copyist 3, 5, 32, 37, 40
Corsica 116
    Royal Corsican Regiment 5
Cowdrey, Mary Bartlett 130n.37
cows
    on the Battery 134n.58
    without horns 80
"Creoles"
    female stagecoach passenger 24, 83
    Native American children 96
criminal identification procedure 122n.32
criminal justice
    in America 76–7
    Maritime Tribunal 116
currency and exchange rate 71–2
customs (excise and duty) in New York 1, 57, 58–9
customs (traditional habits)
    absence of urination in street 67, 86
    masculine dining 67–8
    open-door policy 63–4
    servants served by masters 74–5

de Soldati, Mr. (visitor) 64
debtors: clemency for 77
Declaration of Independence engraving 37–9, 64–5, *65*, 66
Delacroix, Joseph: Vauxhall Gardens 75–6, 132–3n.53
Delaware River 102
Delpino, Caterina *see* Gandolfi, Caterina
Demopolis, Alabama 138n.102
Diani, Teresa (companion) 1, 25, 39, 57, 78, 110, 117
    determination to accompany Mauro 23, 50, 52
    leaves Mauro on return 43
Dickens, Charles 1
Dickinson, Mr. (miniaturist) 64
dining in America 61, 68, 91
dolphins 54
Domenican order 14–15
Dongan, Colonel Thomas 140n.110
Draper, John 37, 91
dress
    of Broadway promenaders 128n.24
    elegance of farmers 81
    on meeting president 133n.55
    of Native Americans 96–7
    of Quakers 91–2, *92*
Durand, Asher B. 141n.117
    Ariadne Asleep on Naxos 27, 124n.72, 130n.36
    Declaration of Independence 39, *65*
Durrant, Mr. 61
Durrell, William 129n.29

Eakins, Thomas 31
Elizabeth, New Jersey 102
English fleet at Gibraltar 114–15
engraving *see* reproductive engraving
epidemics 101, 113, 114
equator 100–01
Erie, Lake 104
etching: Mauro as printmaker 19–20, *21*, 32, 34–5
exchange rates 71–2
Exmouth, Admiral (Edward Pellew, 1st Viscount) 115

Fairman, Gideon 31, 37, 91
Fairmount waterworks, Philadelphia 24–5, 93, *94*, 95
Fancelli, Pietro 18
farming in America
    climate and land 72
    elegant dress of farmers 81
    fencing techniques 82
    fertilizer technique 81
    fruit production 82
    livestock farming 80, 82
figure study
    disregard for in America 30, 31, 90–91
    Mauro as director of 11, 19, 31

see also nude in art
Fillette, Madame (landlady) 88, 91, 139n.102
fires
    Masonic Hall in Philadelphia *99*
    wooden buildings in New York 78, *79*
firewood production 81–2
First Chestnut Street Theater, Philadelphia 88, 137n.84
fishing at sea 54, 55, 56, 109–10
flag of Cispadane Republic 17
Florence: Mauro in 39–40
Floridas 60, 108, 128n.15
flying fish 110
Fogg Museum 123n.60
food: disregard for in America 68
forestry 81–2
Fornasari, Giorgio 41–2
Fourth of July celebrations 8, 25, 73–5, 141n.117
France
    "gallomania" in America 128n.23
    Mauro's early flight to 5–6
    Mauro's journey en route to Bordeaux 23, 51
    see also French-speaking immigrants; Napoleon 1
Franklin, Benjamin 73
    engraved portrait 34
Free-Masons in Philadelphia 98, *99*
freedom of American life
    civil liberty 59–60
    religious tolerance 25–6, 98–100, 102–3
French-speaking immigrants 3, 53, 75, 81, 103, 120n.12
    carnival proposals 75
    fortunes of 92–3
    misfortunes of 69
    as restaurant owners 61, 91
fruit production 82
Fulton, Robert 101
Fulton the First steamboat *101*

"gallomania" 128n.23
Gandolfi, Caterina (*née* Delpino)(second wife) 19, 20,
    22, 41, 42–3, 44, 49
Gandolfi, Clementina (daughter) 2, 9, 11, *11*, 20, 23, 43
    artistic skills 122n.30&34
    marriages 121–2n.30
Gandolfi, Damiano I (brother) 120n.13
Gandolfi, Damiano II (brother) 6, 120n.13
Gandolfi, Democrito (son) 19, 42, 43, 44
    eulogy to father 123n.53
Gandolfi, Emidio (brother) 6, 120n.13, 123n.52
Gandolfi, Gaetano (father) 3, 44
    as artist 3, 5, 11, 14, 121n.24, 122n.40
    Portrait of Mauro 4
    St. Cecilia Seated at the Organ 27, *28*, 129n.26
Gandolfi, Giovanna (*née* Spisani) (mother) 3

Gandolfi, Laura (*née* Zanetti) (first wife) 9, 11, 120n.17
Gandolfi, Marta (sister) 6, 120n.13
Gandolfi, Martino (brother) 6, 120n.13
Gandolfi, Mauro (1764–1834) *4*, *12*, *13*
    artistic career: beginning of 3, 5; carriage decoration
        6, 8, *9*, 33; Cispadane Republic uniform and flag
        designs 17; copying skill 3, 5, 31–2, 37, 40; declines
        Declaration of Independence commission 38–9, 64–5;
        duration 11, 16; exhibited works 27, 89–90, 130n.32,
        142n.119; formal training 8–9, 20, 32; nude skills 9,
        30; opportunities in America 27–8, 30, 31–9, 62–3,
        64–5, 91, 107; painting studio in Bologna 6;
        portraiture skills 33, 40–41; as printmaker 19–20,
        21, 34–5, 91; religious commissions 11, 14–16; as
        reproductive engraver 20, *21*, 23, 31–9, 40; as
        spectacle director 17, 18; *tabbacchiera* designs 40
    artistic works: carriage panels *8*, *9*; *The Christ Child
        Sleeping* 40; *The Cistern of the Palazzo Pubblico* 6;
        Clementina 11; *Eight Fantastic Heads* 22; *The
        Farewell* 6, *7*; *The Happy Dream* 28, *29*, 30, 63; *The
        Healing Vision of St. Pellegrino Laziosi* 15, *16*; *Judith
        with the Head of Holophernes 21*; *Love Sleeping* 40,
        41; *Major Andrew Jackson* engraving 33, *34*; "Moses
        Recovered from the Nile" 66; *Portrait of Anton
        van Leeuwenhoek* 33, *35*; *Portrait of Pelagio Palagi*
        33, *36*; *Republica Cisalpina 17*; *St. Cecilia Seated at
        the Organ* 27, *28*, 63, 89–90; *St. Dominic Burning
        the Books* 14, *15*; *St. Francis and the Pilgrims* 15, *15*;
        Seated male nude 10; self-portraits 11, *12*, *13*
    autobiography 2, 3, 6, 9, 11
    biographical background 3–4
    cemetery plans 18
    character 3, 11, 39–40, 44–5
    civic duties in Bologna 18–19
    early love 5
    escape to France 5–6
    final years and death 43–4
    houses and gardens 22–3, 40, 43
    on human nature 2, 49
    language skills 3, 16–17
    marriage, first 9, 11, 120n.17
    marriage, second 19, 22, 42–3, 44, 49
    mineralogy interest 22–3, 40, 42, 92–3, 113
    musical skills and appreciation 3, 11, 106–7
    natural history interest 22–3, 24, 25, 54, 80, 93–4, 96,
        109–10, 113, 114
    political beliefs and activities 2, 5–6, 16–19, 23, 122n.33
    public scandal 19, 22–3, 41, 42–3, 49
    testamento 28, 40, 44, 124nn.60, 73, 126n.109
    on travel 41–2, 49
    voyage to America: account of *see* "Voyage to the
        United States" *below*; artistic opportunities 27–8,
        30, 31–9, 62–3, 64–5, 91, 107; contract and cost of
        passages 1, 39–40, 52, 109, 117; decision to leave
        and embarkation 1, 22–3, 49–50, 51–3;
        disembarkation and customs in New York 1, 57,
        58–9; length of journey 117; lodgings in New York
        61, 63, 64; name alteration 1, 57–8; nostalgia for 41;
        outward passage 53–7; passport 53; patronage
        unforthcoming 24; reception in society 3, 24, 44,
        96, 142n.119; return passage 39, 108–18; ship life
        53–4, 110–12; storms at sea 24, 55, 110–11, 112, 116–17
    "Voyage to the United States" 1–2, 47–118; dedicatory
        overleaf 126n.1; form and composition 3;
        manuscript copy 2, 119n.4, 126–7n.1; transcription
        and publication 2, 126n.1
Gandolfi, Protasio (brother) 6, 42, 119n.7, 120n.13
Gandolfi, Raffaele (son) 9, 42
gardens
    botanical gardens 25, 33, 95–6
    of Philadelphia houses 87
    pleasure gardens 75–6, 132–3n.53
Garonne river 51
Gazzetta di Milano 42
Gazzetta Privilegiata di Bologna 42
gem-dealing 22–3, 40, 42, 92–3
Gibraltar 39, 109
    English fleet at 114–15
    flora and fauna 113, 114
    treacherous sailors 115–16
Gimbrede, Thomas 33, *34*, 64, 107
Gonfalionieri 8
Gorgogne rock 116
Gothic architecture *99*, 102
Gradual Manumission Act (1799) 131–2n.48
Graff, Frederick 139n.104
grafting procedure 81–2
Grassili, Giuseppe 121n.30
Great Lakes of America 104
Gualandi, Michelangelo 2, 126nn.109, 1, 137n.86
Gualdo, John 126n.112
Guidicini, Giuseppe 43, 122n.43, 123n.50

Hall, Lieutenant Francis 128n.24, 142n.118
Hamilton, Andrew 137n.86
Havana, Cuba 101
Hayward, George *61*
healthy eating: unheard of in America 68
Heath, Charles 38, 138n.97
Hicks, Edward 26
Hill, John *57*, *74*, *99*
Hills, The, Philadelphia 139n.107
history painting 30, 37–9
Holland, John Joseph *58*
honesty of Americans 25, 52, 87
    merchandise on display 76

open door custom 63–4
horseshoe crabs 109–10
hospitals in America 76–7
Hyde de Neuville family *53*
    see also Rouillé de Marigny, Anne-Marguérite-
        Henriette
hydraulic machines 93, 95

icebergs 56
Illinois tribe 80, 96–7
immigrants in America 25, 44, 60, 88
    Irish immigrants 25, 76, 127n.3
    see also French-speaking immigrants
Institute for Science and the Arts, Bologna 20
intaglio techniques 32
Irish immigrants 25, 76, 127n.3
Iroquois tribe 80, 97–8, *97*
Irving, Washington 137n.85, 143n.122
Italy
    disgraceful practices at home 86
    immigrants in America 25
    Napoleonic incursions 16–19, 23, 121n.22

Jackson, Andrew: engraved portrait 33, *34*, 64
Jane Shore (tragedy) 104, *105*
Jefferson, Thomas 37, 73
jewellers *see* gem-dealing
Jews of Armenia 117–18
Jones, Samuel *99*
Juliani, Richard 126n.112

kelp 54
Killing No Murder (musical comedy) 104, 106–7
Klinckowström, Baron Axel Leonhard
    American scenes *56, 73, 95*
    on Broadway fashion 128n.24
    on "colored race" 132n.49
    on disregard for food 131n.42
    on dress for meeting president 133n.55
    on Fourth of July celebrations 133n.53
    on Schuylkill bridge 139n.106
    on waterworks 139n.103
Kneass, William *99*
Krimmel, John Lewis *99*

Languedoc canal 51
Latrobe, Benjamin Henry 133n.54, 136nn.77, 80,
    139n.104
Lawson, A. *95*
Lazzaretto of S. Giacomo 117–18
Leeuwenhoek, Antony van 33, *35*
Leghorn 116
Leney, William Satchwell 33, 64, 131n.39

Leslie, C. R. 90
life drawing in America 30, 31, 91
lightning threat 112
line etching 19, 32, 35
Linnaean classification 24, 96
lithography 32, 130nn.33, 34
livestock
    drinking curtailed on board ship 111–12
    farming 80, 82
    in public places 134n.58
Logan, Mrs. (Deborah Norris) 120n.12
Louvre, Chalcographie du 20
Low, John 129n.29
Lutherans 99–100
Lyon 51

macaque monkeys 114
McComb, John 133n.54
Madison, James 60
Main, William 39–40, 64, 108–9
Maison Carrée, Nimes 51
Mangin, Joseph-François 133n.54, 141n.113
"manikin": confounds Americans 59
Marble, Joseph 126n.112
Marescalchi, Ferdinando 125n.79
marine life 54, 109–10
Maritime Tribunal 116
market in Philadelphia 87–8, *87*
Marseilles 5
Martinetti, Madame 109
masks prohibition of 75
Masonic Hall, Philadelphia 98, *99*
mastodon skeleton 88
medal commemorating abolition 70
Mediterranean: prone to storms 50, 109
Mexican insurrection 101
Milan
    climate in 72
    Mauro as engraver in 40, 42
    Mauro meets Teresa in 23, 50
Minozzi, Flaminio 18
Mississippi land sale 93
Mitchill, Dr. Samuel Latham 64
money system of America 71–2
monkeys on Gibraltar 114
Monroe, James 60, 107, 108, 133n.55
Montecuccoli, Carlo Caprara 6, 17
Montpellier 51
Morghern, Van (engraver) 39–40
Morocco 113, 114
Morris, Robert 95, 96
Murray, George 31, 37, 91
Murray, John R. 64, 74, 142n.119

Musée de la Révolution, Paris 20
Musée des Voitures, Compiègne 121n.23
Musée Français/Musée Royal 20, 37, 40
museums 123n.60
    American Museum of Natural Science 142n.118
    Peale Museum, Philadelphia 88–9

Napoleon I, emperor of France 16–19, 23, 43, 121n.22,
    136n.76
Native Americans 25, 80, *89*, 96–8, *97*
    "Creole" stagecoach passenger 24, 83
    dress 96–7
    sale of land 93
natural history
    of America 80, 93–4
    American Museum of Natural Science 142n.118
    of Gibraltar 113, 114
    Linnaean classification 24, 96
    in Philadelphia museum 88–9
    products of the sea 54, 109–10
Neagle, J. 141n.117
"Negro plot" (1741) 140n.113
negroes *see* black people
Nemours, Dupont de 3
New York
    architectural styles 24, 57, *58*, 78, *79*
    arrival in 1, 56–9
    art in 107–8, 129n.30
    black people in 69–71
    climate 72
    exhibition rooms 107–8
    fires in 78, *79*
    first Catholic church 102–3
    Fourth of July celebrations 8, 25, 73–5, 141n.117
    French-speaking immigrants 53, 69, 75, 103, 120n.12
    lodgings in 61, 63, 64
    pigs at large *73*, *81*, 136n.73
    theater in 39, 104–7, *106*
New York Academy of the Arts of Design 129n.30
New York Academy of Fine Arts 26, 107, 129n.30
New York Evening Post 132n.53, 134n.58, 141nn.113, 116,
    141–2n.117
New York Gazette 119n.3
New York Gazette and General Advertiser 133n.53
New York Historical Society 125n.90, 130n.31&34,
    142n.118
New York Institution of Learned and Scientific
    Establishments 142n.118
New York Literary and Philosophical Society 142n.118
New York Public Library 123n.60
New York Society Library 142n.118
Newark, New Jersey 80

Newfoundland 55–6
Newton, Gilbert Stuart 90
Niagara Falls 103–4
Nîmes 51
Noble Savage 25
nude in art
    American aversion to 26–7, 30, 31, 83, 89–90, 91, 107
    Mauro excels at 9, 30

Ontario, Lake 104
open-door custom 63–4
Opere Pie 16
oysters as foodstuff 69, 70

Paff, Michael A. 64
Palagi, Pelagio 33, *36*, 119n.7, 138n.92
Palazzo Bentivoglio, Bologna 6, 43
Palazzo Comunale, Bologna 19–20
Palma, John (di) 126n.112
Palmer, John
    on accounts of America 119n.5
    on almshouse 135n.64
    on antipathy towards Native Americans 140n.108
    on capital punishment 134n.62
    on City Hall 133n.54
    on pigs in New York 136n.73
    on prostitution 131n.41
    on travellers' meals 131n.43
    on wooden buildings 136n.79
Palmer, Samuel 34
Paris: Mauro's training in 5–6, 20, 32
Park Theater, New York 104–7, *106*, 141nn.115, 116
Partition Street, New York 63
Peale, Charles Willson 3, 30, 33–4, 137n.87
Peale Museum, Philadelphia 88–9
Pedrini, Filippo 18
penitentiaries in America 76–7, *78*
Penn, William 25, 84
    see also Quakers
Pennsylvania Academy of Fine Arts 27, 30, 31–2, 89–90,
    90
Perkins, Jacob 108, 138n.97
Perpignan, Stephen 61
Peyrou gateway, Montpellier 52
Philadelphia 25, 78, 83–100
    Academy of Fine Arts 27, 30, 31–2, 89–90, *90*
    architecture and city design 84–5, *84*, *85*, 86–7, *86*, *87*,
    88, *89*
    art in 88–90
    botanical gardens 25, 95–6
    churches 98–100
    climate 88

French-speaking community 3, 91, 92–3
history of 83–4
journey by stagecoach 78, 80, 82–3, 102
lodgings in 88
market 87–8, *87*
natural history museum 88–9
Quakers 84, 88, 91–2, 98–9
Schuylkill suburb 93–6, *94, 95*
theater 88
waterworks 24–5, 93, *94, 95*
Philadelphia Museum of Art 123n.60
Piazzetta, Giambattista 121n.25
pigs at large *73, 81,* 136n.73
Pinacoteca Nazionale di Bologna 11
Pintard, John 24, 64, 133n.55, 137n.87
Pius VII, pope 140n.113
plague in Gibraltar 113
plants 22–3, 54, 80, 96, 113, 114
pleasure gardens 75–6, 132–3n.53
policemen in New York 75, 76
Ponte, Lorenzo da 44
portraiture
    engravings 33–9
    in Philadelphia 90
Portuguese man o'war 54
Poussin, Nicolas 90
Pratt, Henry 139–40n.107
Pratt, Matthew 139n.107
presidential system 60
printmaking
    lack of opportunity in America 35, 37
    Mauro's training 19–20, 32
    status in America 34–5, 91
    techniques for 32
    see also reproductive engraving
prisons in America 76–7, *78*
products of the sea 54, 109–10
prostitutes: lack of demand 68
prudery 67
    aversion to nudity 26–7, 30, 31, 83, 89–90, 91, 107
public gardens 75–6, 132–3n.53
Puglia, James Philip 126n.112

Quakers 25–6, 143n.63
    dress 91–2, *92*
    masculine dining 67–8
    in Philadelphia 84, 88, 91–2, 98–9
    views on art 26, 66
quarantine station 117–18

Rae, Captain 109, 112, 114, 116–17
Raphael: *St. Cecilia* 129n.26, 130n.36

religious art: decline in Italy 11, 14–16
religious tolerance in America 25–6, 98–100, 102–3
Reni, Guido: *Madonna and Child* 27, 89, 142n.119
reproductive engraving 20, 32, 108
    for banknotes 37, 131n.38, 138n.97, 143n.123
    Declaration of Independence 37–9, 64–5, *65, 66*
    Mauro's training 20, 32
    in Milan 40
    opportunities in America 31–9, 64–5, 91, 107
    portrait engravings 33–9
republicanism
    in America 25
    Brutus as symbol of 132n.51
    Mauro's hopes for Italy 2, 5–6, 16–19, 23, 43, 122n.33
restaurants in America 61, 91
resto del carlino, Il (newspaper) 2
revolutionary ephemera 17
Reynolds, Sir Joshua 90
Rhône river 51
Ricci, Sebastiano 121n.25
ritrattini 41
Riva Reno house 43
Robertson, Andrew 38
Robertson, Archibald 33, 64
Rosapina, Francesco 123n.56
Rouillé de Marigny, Anne-Marguérite-Henriette *53, 78, 79, 81,* 97
Royal Canadian Mounted Police 122n.32
Royal Corsican Regiment 5
Rymsdyk, Jan van 137n.90

St. Patrick's cathedral, New York 140–41nn.113, 114
Sargasso Sea 127n.5
Savoy Alps 23, 50–51
Scarabelli, Luciano 2, 5, 22–3, 40, 44–5, 123n.60, 126n.1
Schuylkill suburb, Philadelphia 93–6, *94, 95*
sea life 54, 109–10
sea swallows 110
Searle, John *106*
seasickness remedies 5, 110–11
seaweed 54
Sedazzi, Luigi 33, 40, 42, 124n.73, 138nn.92, 101
Select Review 137n.85
servants served by masters custom 74–5
Sharp, William 64
shipwreck threat 116–17
shops
    market in Philadelphia 87–8, *87*
    merchandise on display 76
shot tower *94*
siderography 108
slavery: abolition 70–71, 131–2n.48

Smith, Richard 134n.63
Snyder, Governor 134n.63
Society of Artists, Philadelphia 30, 31
Spain
    legacy on Gibraltar 113
    possessions in America 128n.15
speculation 24, 26, 69, 92
    leads to bankruptcies 77–8
Spencer, Asa 138n.97
Spisani, Giovanna *see* Gandolfi, Giovanna
stagecoach travel 78, 80, 82–3, 102
Stansbury, Arthur J. 64
Stati delle anime 120n.13
"Statuto Costituzionale" 19
Stauffer, David McNeely 125n.90, 138n.91
steam pumps 93, 95
steamboat travel 101–2, *101*, 103–4
Stendhal (Henri Beyle) 23
Sterling, Mr. (visitor) 64
storms at sea 24, 55, 110–11, 112, 116–17
    in Mediterranean 50
Strickland, William *99*
Sully, Thomas 3, 31

tabbacchiera designs 40
Tanari family 8
Tanner, Benjamin *90, 101*
Teatro Comunale, Bologna 39
Thackara, James 31, 89, 90–91
Thackara, William 138n.91
theater
    in New York 39, 104–7, *106*
    in Philadelphia 88
Thomas, Moses 88, 129n.29
thunderbolts 112
Tocqueville, Alexis de 1–2, 24
Tomlinson, Ebenezer 137n.86
Tommasi, Gaetano 43
Tompkins, Daniel D. ("Tonchins") (Governor of New York) 60, 75
Tonini, Luigi 122n.40
Toulouse 51
tower of lead 94
"transparencies" 132–3nn.52, 53
trees 80, 81–2, 86
Trenton wooden bridge 82–3
Trollope, Frances 1, 139n.104
Trumbull, John 130n.31
    Declaration of Independence 37–9, 64, *65*
Turin 50
turtle dove 112–13
Twain, Mark 139n.104

Ubaldo 120n.16
uniform of Cispadane Republic 17
urination in streets 67, 86

vaglio, Il (literary newspaper) 2
Vallardi, Pietro and Giuseppe 40, 120n.14
Vanderlyn, John 64, 107, 143n.121
    Ariadne Asleep on Naxos 26–7, *27*, 107, 130n.36
Vauxhall Gardens, New York 75–6, 132–3n.53
Vecchio, C. D. 28, 61–3, 103
Vespucci, Amerigo 73
Vien, Joseph-Marie 27

Wall, William Guy *57, 74*
Wandolf, Giulio Nilo (Giulietto) 126n.109
Washington, George 73
Washington: seat of government 60
waterspouts 112
waterworks in Philadelphia 24–5, 93, *94*, 95
Wertmüller, Adolph-Ulric: *Danae and the Golden Rain* 27
West, Benjamin 37, 38, 90, 129n.30
whales 54
Whelan, Charles 140n.113
William and Henry (merchant brigadier) 1, 52, 53–4
William Street, New York 61, *61*
wine
    in America 26, 61
    on board ship 56
women
    beauty of American 66, 67
    black women laundresses 71
    "Creole" stagecoach passenger 24, 83
    hardship of Native American 97
    kept from male company 67–8
    low number of prostitutes 68
Wood, Samuel 131nn.46, 47, 135n.68
wooden bridges 82–3, 94–5, *95*
Wooley, Edmund 137n.86

xenophobia in America 44, 88

Yellow Fever epidemic 101

Zanetti, Laura *see* Gandolfi, Laura
Zanotti, Dr. Augusto 2
Zanotti, Onofrio 121–2n.30
Zecchi, Giovanni 18, 124n.60